Wise Guys

100 Days on the Road to Wisdom

by
Jeff Hendley

Library of Congress
Control Number: 2005900529

ISBN 0-9762014-1-0

Published by L'Edge Press
A division of Upside Down Ministries, Inc.
Boone, North Carolina

Translations

I have chosen to use various translations and paraphrases to help in the reading and understanding of these passages. If you have a favorite translation, then just turn to the passage in your Bible and read it from that translation.

The Old Testament was written in Hebrew and the New Testament was written in Greek. In fact, the Greek language of the New Testament was the "market" language of that time. This means it was the street language or the everyday language that the people used to speak to one another.

Therefore, it helps us to understand what the Bible is saying when we take the original Hebrew and Greek and translate it into our everyday language that we use to communicate. These various translations in this journal are a reflection of the translations that have been done over the past decades.

Wise Guys...A note from Jeff

Years ago someone suggested that I read one chapter of Proverbs a day. By doing so I could work my way through Proverbs each month and twelve times per year. I took the challenge. Even though I was not consistent I started reading Proverbs. I used the day of the month to tell me what chapter to read. Even after all the journeys through Proverbs I am still fascinated by what Proverbs teaches about Wisdom. I used different translations and paraphrases to gain fresh insight about the proverbs.

Wisdom is available. Just think, the same Wisdom that created the world in the beginning of time is the same Wisdom that you and I can have. This Wisdom can help us make decisions, protect us from evil, help us overcome lust and teach us about living a godly life. This Wisdom gives us an edge in family life, in marriage, in business, and in relationships. This Wisdom can keep us from following the wrong path and can teach us how to be successful in any endeavor in life. This Wisdom can and will teach us how to be successful in whatever we do—whether it be friendships, marriage, business, government, education, or being a student. Wisdom has application to anything and everything we do.

It is not a get-rich-quick scheme. In other words, it is not a magic pill to take to be successful. But the teachings of Wisdom will lead us to a life lived before God and before others in such a way as to bring honor and glory to God.

Wisdom can be acquired. It can be asked for. It can be found. It can be hunted as treasure. It is to be sought after above all else. It calls to us and beckons to us. Wisdom wants to be found and we can find her. Solomon tells his son that even though it cost him all he has to get wisdom and understanding.

I invite you to join me on this journey to get wisdom and understanding—no matter what it cost. I invite you to read about Wisdom and to do the things Wisdom says do. It is an adventure. It is a treasure hunt. It is a mystery to be solved. It is wild and crazy. Wisdom can be found and the same Wisdom that founded the universe, the same Wisdom that Jesus had is the same Wisdom that can be ours. *Let's go for it.*

Introduction

God invites us into a personal relationship with Himself. Just think! We can have a personal relationship with the God of creation. *It is His idea!*

When Jesus chose His twelve disciples, He made a statement that sheds light on this invitation to a relationship, "*Jesus went up on a mountainside and called to him those he wanted and they came to him...that they might be with him.*" Mark 3:13-14, NIV

In the book of Acts, Peter and John had gotten into a bit of trouble for talking about Jesus after He had died and ascended to Heaven. They also performed a miracle and healed a man crippled for years. Of course, the religious leaders did not take this kindly, so they had Peter and John put into prison. The next day they were dragged into court to testify before all the religious biggies. Listen to what was recorded after they spoke, "*When they saw the courage of Peter and John and realized that they were unschooled, ordinary men, they were astonished and they took note that these men had been with Jesus.*" Acts 4:13, NIV

The unbelievable reality of this relationship is that God wants us to be with Him. He invites us. We do not have to force it. We do not have to do anything to be invited. We are welcomed into God's presence by His invitation. Naturally, the focal point of our lives should be this relationship with God.

> "*Jesus answered, 'Love the Lord your God with all your heart, all your soul, and all your mind. This is the first and most important command.'*
> *And the second command is like the first: Love your neighbor as you love yourself. All the law and the writings of the prophets depend on these two commands.*" Matthew 22:37-40 NCV

Life is all about relationships. Relationships with those around us. A relationship with our own selves. And a relationship with God. Since God is Spirit, this relationship takes on a tad bit of difference.

"Human life comes from the human parents, but spiritual life comes from the Spirit."…."God is spirit, and those who worship him must worship in spirit and truth." John 3:6, John 4:24 NCV

The spiritual world is as real as the physical world. But we are not used to dealing with spiritual things so we have to focus a bit more if we are to have a "spiritual relationship" with God.

If we want to pursue this relationship with God we can do so just like we would pursue any relationship that is meaningful. It will take time, energy, and commitment—all geared to getting to know each other.

Wise Guys is a tool. It is a tool to help establish a habit of spending a few moments with God during the day. It is designed to bring us into direct contact with the words God has spoken.

There are two assumptions that are being made before starting to use *Wise Guys*:

1. That 2 Corinthians 5:17-18 is a reality in our lives:

    "For if a person is in Christ he becomesa new person altogether—the past is finished and gone, everything has become fresh and new. All this is God's doing…" Phillips

2. That there is a desire to have a close relationship with God.

Below are a few hints that will better prepare us for our time with God:

1. Find a place where you can be alone and quiet.

2. Find a time where you can spend a few moments with God. It can be anytime: morning, mid-morning, afternoon, evening, etc.

3. Be consistent but do not get hung up on the "everyday" notion. It would be great if you established a daily pattern but that's not important right now. The *Wise Guys* devotional is designed so you can go at your own pace and when you want to get away for a few minutes.

4. Navigating through *Wise Guys*

A. Each day there is one chapter of Proverbs or another passage of Scripture that talks about wisdom. The daily reading is listed at the beginning of the journal. Proverbs 1-31 are taken entirely from the NIV Translation.

B. The journaling part is divided into three sections:

1) *What stands out? A thought, a word, a phrase.* If something strikes you in your reading then highlight it and record your thoughts.

2) *What can be worked on today?* Here is a chance to put into practice something God is trying to bring to your attention. Jot down your thoughts and make it as practical as you can. For example: Proverbs 10:19, "When words are many, sin is not absent." God may use these words to tell us to talk less and listen more. Sometimes we talk too much and let our tongues get us into trouble. Listen more, talk less. This can be the practical thing God wants us to work on for that day.

3) *What are you thinking, dreaming, praying?* Use this space to record what is going through your mind, what is on your heart or what you may be dreaming about. It may be an idea waiting to be hatched. It could be something you are praying about or someone you are praying for.

C. More Space.

As you journey through this journal you may find yourself saying exactly what one of my boys said recently; "Dad, there is not enough space to write down everything on my mind." If so, feel free to use a notebook to expand your journaling.

D. Who Knows?

It will not be long before you realize that God is using His word to teach you about life and yourself. There will be patterns that will emerge. Creative ideas popping out. Subjects to explore. Sins to confess. Ideas to share.

Who knows? You may even find yourself writing poems, birthing songs, or even beginning the lines of a book God wants you to write.

E. Keep at it.

The key is to keep going until you complete the journey.

F. The Fellowship of Wisdom.

Find a couple of friends that will do this with you. You may even want to meet weekly to explore together what God is teaching you about WISDOM.

Oswald Chambers, *My Utmost for His Highest,* is a terrific devotional. I have listed several quotes from this book so you can read some of the things he said over 100 years ago.

"It is not practical activities that are the strength of this Training College…its whole strength lies in the fact you are put here to soak before God…but if this time of soaking before God is being spent in getting rooted and grounded in God…you will remain true to Him whatever happens."

"Have I a personal history with Jesus Christ? The one sign of discipleship is intimate connection with Him, a knowledge of Jesus Christ which nothing can shake."

"The measure of the worth of our public activity for God is private and profound communion we have with Him...We have to pitch our tents where we shall always have quiet times with God, however noisy our times with the world may be."

"There is nothing there apart from the personal relationship. Paul was devoted to a Person not a cause. He was absolutely Jesus Christ's, he saw nothing else, he lived for nothing else."

"If you want to be of use to God, get rightly related to Jesus Christ and He will make you of use unconsciously every minute you live."

"It is the innermost of the innermost that reveals the power of life...The central thing about the Kingdom of Jesus Christ is a personal relationship to Himself, not public usefulness to men...but if this time of soaking before God is being spent rooted and grounded in God...you will remain true to him no matter what happens."

"The whole discipline of life is to enable us to enter into this closest relationship with Jesus Christ...When once we get intimate with Jesus we are never lonely, we never need sympathy, we can pour out all the time...."

My prayer for each of us is that this time of "soaking before God" will enable us to enjoy a personal, intimate relationship with Jesus Christ.

Wise Guys

100 Days on the Road to Wisdom

Proverbs 1

[1] The proverbs of Solomon son of David, king of Israel:

[2] for attaining wisdom and discipline;
for understanding words of insight;
[3] for acquiring a disciplined and prudent life,
doing what is right and just and fair;
[4] for giving prudence to the simple,
knowledge and discretion to the young-
[5] let the wise listen and add to their learning,
and let the discerning get guidance-
[6] for understanding proverbs and parables,
the sayings and riddles of the wise.

[7] The fear of the Lord is the beginning of knowledge,
but fools despise wisdom and discipline.

[8] Listen, my son, to your father's instruction
and do not forsake your mother's teaching.
[9] They will be a garland to grace your head
and a chain to adorn your neck.

[10] My son, if sinners entice you,
do not give in to them.
[11] If they say, "Come along with us;
let's lie in wait for someone's blood,
let's waylay some harmless soul;
[12] let's swallow them alive, like the grave,
and whole, like those who go down to the pit;
[13] we will get all sorts of valuable things
and fill our houses with plunder;
[14] throw in your lot with us,
and we will share a common purse"-
[15] my son, do not go along with them,
do not set foot on their paths;
[16] for their feet rush into sin,
they are swift to shed blood
[17] How useless to spread a net
in full view of all the birds!

[18] These men lie in wait for their own blood;
they waylay only themselves!
[19] Such is the end of all who go after ill-gotten gain;
it takes away the lives of those who get it.

[20] Wisdom calls aloud in the street,
she raises her voice in the public squares;
[21] at the head of the noisy streets she cries out,
in the gateways of the city she makes her speech:

[22] "How long will you simple ones love your simple ways?
How long will mockers delight in mockery
and fools hate knowledge?
[23] If you had responded to my rebuke,
I would have poured out my heart to you
and made my thoughts known to you.
[24] But since you rejected me when I called
and no one gave heed when I stretched out my hand,
[25] since you ignored all my advice
and would not accept my rebuke,
[26] I in turn will laugh at your disaster;
I will mock when calamity overtakes you-
[27] when calamity overtakes you like a storm,
when disaster sweeps over you like a whirlwind,
when distress and trouble overwhelm you.

[28] "Then they will call to me but I will not answer;
they will look for me but will not find me.
[29] Since they hated knowledge
and did not choose to fear the LORD,
[30] since they would not accept my advice
and spurned my rebuke,
[31] they will eat the fruit of their ways
and be filled with the fruit of their schemes.
[32] For the waywardness of the simple will kill them,
and the complacency of fools will destroy them;
[33] but whoever listens to me will live in safety
and be at ease, without fear of harm."

Proverbs 2

[1] My son, if you accept my words
and store up my commands within you,
[2] turning your ear to wisdom
and applying your heart to understanding,
[3] and if you call out for insight
and cry aloud for understanding,
[4] and if you look for it as for silver
and search for it as for hidden treasure,
[5] then you will understand the fear of the LORD
and find the knowledge of God.
[6] For the LORD gives wisdom,
and from his mouth come knowledge and understanding.
[7] He holds victory in store for the upright,
he is a shield to those whose walk is blameless,
[8] for he guards the course of the just
and protects the way of his faithful ones.
[9] Then you will understand what is right and just
and fair-every good path.
[10] For wisdom will enter your heart,
and knowledge will be pleasant to your soul.
[11] Discretion will protect you,
and understanding will guard you.

[12] Wisdom will save you from the ways of wicked men,
from men whose words are perverse,
[13] who leave the straight paths
to walk in dark ways,
[14] who delight in doing wrong
and rejoice in the perverseness of evil,
[15] whose paths are crooked
and who are devious in their ways.

[16] It will save you also from the adulteress,
from the wayward wife with her seductive words,
[17] who has left the partner of her youth
and ignored the covenant she made before God.
[18] For her house leads down to death
and her paths to the spirits of the dead.

¹⁹ None who go to her return
or attain the paths of life.

²⁰ Thus you will walk in the ways of good men
and keep to the paths of the righteous.
²¹ For the upright will live in the land,
and the blameless will remain in it;
²² but the wicked will be cut off from the land,
and the unfaithful will be torn from it.

Proverbs 3

¹ My son, do not forget my teaching,
but keep my commands in your heart,
² for they will prolong your life many years
and bring you prosperity.

³ Let love and faithfulness never leave you;
bind them around your neck,
write them on the tablet of your heart.
⁴ Then you will win favor and a good name
in the sight of God and man.

⁵ Trust in the LORD with all your heart
and lean not on your own understanding;
⁶ in all your ways acknowledge him,
and he will make your paths straight.

⁷ Do not be wise in your own eyes;
fear the LORD and shun evil.
⁸ This will bring health to your body
and nourishment to your bones.

⁹ Honor the LORD with your wealth,
with the firstfruits of all your crops;
¹⁰ then your barns will be filled to overflowing,
and your vats will brim over with new wine.

¹¹ My son, do not despise the LORD's discipline
and do not resent his rebuke,

¹² because the LORD disciplines those he loves,
as a father the son he delights in.

¹³ Blessed is the man who finds wisdom,
the man who gains understanding,
¹⁴ for she is more profitable than silver
and yields better returns than gold.
¹⁵ She is more precious than rubies;
nothing you desire can compare with her.
¹⁶ Long life is in her right hand;
in her left hand are riches and honor.
¹⁷ Her ways are pleasant ways,
and all her paths are peace.
¹⁸ She is a tree of life to those who embrace her;
those who lay hold of her will be blessed.

¹⁹ By wisdom the LORD laid the earth's foundations,
by understanding he set the heavens in place;
²⁰ by his knowledge the deeps were divided,
and the clouds let drop the dew.

²¹ My son, preserve sound judgment and discernment,
do not let them out of your sight;
²² they will be life for you,
an ornament to grace your neck.
²³ Then you will go on your way in safety,
and your foot will not stumble;
²⁴ when you lie down, you will not be afraid;
when you lie down, your sleep will be sweet.
²⁵ Have no fear of sudden disaster
or of the ruin that overtakes the wicked,
²⁶ for the LORD will be your confidence
and will keep your foot from being snared.

²⁷ Do not withhold good from those who deserve it,
when it is in your power to act.
²⁸ Do not say to your neighbor,
"Come back later; I'll give it tomorrow"-
when you now have it with you.

²⁹ Do not plot harm against your neighbor,
who lives trustfully near you.
³⁰ Do not accuse a man for no reason-
when he has done you no harm.

³¹ Do not envy a violent man
or choose any of his ways,
³² for the LORD detests a perverse man
but takes the upright into his confidence.

³³ The LORD's curse is on the house of the wicked,
but he blesses the home of the righteous.
³⁴ He mocks proud mockers
but gives grace to the humble.
³⁵ The wise inherit honor,
but fools he holds up to shame.

Proverbs 4

¹ Listen, my sons, to a father's instruction;
pay attention and gain understanding.
² I give you sound learning,
so do not forsake my teaching.
³ When I was a boy in my father's house,
still tender, and an only child of my mother,
⁴ he taught me and said,
"Lay hold of my words with all your heart;
keep my commands and you will live.
⁵ Get wisdom, get understanding;
do not forget my words or swerve from them.
⁶ Do not forsake wisdom, and she will protect you;
love her, and she will watch over you.
⁷ Wisdom is supreme; therefore get wisdom.
Though it cost all you have, get understanding.
⁸ Esteem her, and she will exalt you;
embrace her, and she will honor you.
⁹ She will set a garland of grace on your head
and present you with a crown of splendor."

[10] Listen, my son, accept what I say,
and the years of your life will be many.
[11] I guide you in the way of wisdom
and lead you along straight paths.
[12] When you walk, your steps will not be hampered;
when you run, you will not stumble.
[13] Hold on to instruction, do not let it go;
guard it well, for it is your life.
[14] Do not set foot on the path of the wicked
or walk in the way of evil men.
[15] Avoid it, do not travel on it;
turn from it and go on your way.
[16] For they cannot sleep till they do evil;
they are robbed of slumber till they make someone fall.
[17] They eat the bread of wickedness
and drink the wine of violence.
[18] The path of the righteous is like the first gleam of dawn,
shining ever brighter till the full light of day.
[19] But the way of the wicked is like deep darkness;
they do not know what makes them stumble.

[20] My son, pay attention to what I say;
listen closely to my words.
[21] Do not let them out of your sight,
keep them within your heart;
[22] for they are life to those who find them
and health to a man's whole body.
[23] Above all else, guard your heart,
for it is the wellspring of life.
[24] Put away perversity from your mouth;
keep corrupt talk far from your lips.
[25] Let your eyes look straight ahead,
fix your gaze directly before you.
[26] Make level paths for your feet
and take only ways that are firm.
[27] Do not swerve to the right or the left;
keep your foot from evil.

Proverbs 5

[1] My son, pay attention to my wisdom,
listen well to my words of insight,
[2] that you may maintain discretion
and your lips may preserve knowledge.
[3] For the lips of an adulteress drip honey,
and her speech is smoother than oil;
[4] but in the end she is bitter as gall,
sharp as a double-edged sword.
[5] Her feet go down to death;
her steps lead straight to the grave.
[6] She gives no thought to the way of life;
her paths are crooked, but she knows it not.

[7] Now then, my sons, listen to me;
do not turn aside from what I say.
[8] Keep to a path far from her,
do not go near the door of her house,
[9] lest you give your best strength to others
and your years to one who is cruel,
[10] lest strangers feast on your wealth
and your toil enrich another man's house.
[11] At the end of your life you will groan,
when your flesh and body are spent.
[12] You will say, "How I hated discipline!
How my heart spurned correction!
[13] I would not obey my teachers
or listen to my instructors.
[14] I have come to the brink of utter ruin
in the midst of the whole assembly."

[15] Drink water from your own cistern,
running water from your own well.
[16] Should your springs overflow in the streets,
your streams of water in the public squares?
[17] Let them be yours alone,
never to be shared with strangers.
[18] May your fountain be blessed,
and may you rejoice in the wife of your youth.

[19] A loving doe, a graceful deer—
may her breasts satisfy you always,
may you ever be captivated by her love.
[20] Why be captivated, my son, by an adulteress?
Why embrace the bosom of another man's wife?

[21] For a man's ways are in full view of the LORD,
and he examines all his paths.
[22] The evil deeds of a wicked man ensnare him;
the cords of his sin hold him fast.
[23] He will die for lack of discipline,
led astray by his own great folly.

Proverbs 6

[1] My son, if you have put up security for your neighbor,
if you have struck hands in pledge for another,
[2] if you have been trapped by what you said,
ensnared by the words of your mouth,
[3] then do this, my son, to free yourself,
since you have fallen into your neighbor's hands:
Go and humble yourself;
press your plea with your neighbor!
[4] Allow no sleep to your eyes,
no slumber to your eyelids.
[5] Free yourself, like a gazelle from the hand of the hunter,
like a bird from the snare of the fowler.

[6] Go to the ant, you sluggard;
consider its ways and be wise!
[7] It has no commander,
no overseer or ruler,
[8] yet it stores its provisions in summer
and gathers its food at harvest.

[9] How long will you lie there, you sluggard?
When will you get up from your sleep?
[10] A little sleep, a little slumber,
a little folding of the hands to rest—

[11] and poverty will come on you like a bandit
and scarcity like an armed man.

[12] A scoundrel and villain,
who goes about with a corrupt mouth,
[13] who winks with his eye,
signals with his feet and motions with his fingers,
[14] who plots evil with deceit in his heart-
he always stirs up dissension.
[15] Therefore disaster will overtake him in an instant;
he will suddenly be destroyed-without remedy.

[16] There are six things the LORD hates,
seven that are detestable to him:
[17] haughty eyes,
a lying tongue,
hands that shed innocent blood,
[18] a heart that devises wicked schemes,
feet that are quick to rush into evil,
[19] a false witness who pours out lies
and a man who stirs up dissension among brothers.

[20] My son, keep your father's commands
and do not forsake your mother's teaching.
[21] Bind them upon your heart forever;
fasten them around your neck.
[22] When you walk, they will guide you;
when you sleep, they will watch over you;
when you awake, they will speak to you.
[23] For these commands are a lamp,
this teaching is a light,
and the corrections of discipline
are the way to life,
[24] keeping you from the immoral woman,
from the smooth tongue of the wayward wife.
[25] Do not lust in your heart after her beauty
or let her captivate you with her eyes,
[26] for the prostitute reduces you to a loaf of bread,
and the adulteress preys upon your very life.

²⁷ Can a man scoop fire into his lap
without his clothes being burned?
²⁸ Can a man walk on hot coals
without his feet being scorched?
²⁹ So is he who sleeps with another man's wife;
no one who touches her will go unpunished.

³⁰ Men do not despise a thief if he steals
to satisfy his hunger when he is starving.
³¹ Yet if he is caught, he must pay sevenfold,
though it costs him all the wealth of his house.
³² But a man who commits adultery lacks judgment;
whoever does so destroys himself.
³³ Blows and disgrace are his lot,
and his shame will never be wiped away;
³⁴ for jealousy arouses a husband's fury,
and he will show no mercy when he takes revenge.
³⁵ He will not accept any compensation;
he will refuse the bribe, however great it is.

Proverbs 7

¹ My son, keep my words
and store up my commands within you.
² Keep my commands and you will live;
guard my teachings as the apple of your eye.
³ Bind them on your fingers;
write them on the tablet of your heart.
⁴ Say to wisdom, "You are my sister,"
and call understanding your kinsman;
⁵ they will keep you from the adulteress,
from the wayward wife with her seductive words.

⁶ At the window of my house
I looked out through the lattice.
⁷ I saw among the simple,
I noticed among the young men,
a youth who lacked judgment.
⁸ He was going down the street near her corner,
walking along in the direction of her house

⁹ at twilight, as the day was fading,
as the dark of night set in.

¹⁰ Then out came a woman to meet him,
dressed like a prostitute and with crafty intent.
¹¹ (She is loud and defiant,
her feet never stay at home;
¹² now in the street, now in the squares,
at every corner she lurks.)
¹³ She took hold of him and kissed him
and with a brazen face she said:

¹⁴ "I have fellowship offerings at home;
today I fulfilled my vows.
¹⁵ So I came out to meet you;
I looked for you and have found you!
¹⁶ I have covered my bed
with colored linens from Egypt.
¹⁷ I have perfumed my bed
with myrrh, aloes and cinnamon.
¹⁸ Come, let's drink deep of love till morning;
let's enjoy ourselves with love!
¹⁹ My husband is not at home;
he has gone on a long journey.
²⁰ He took his purse filled with money
and will not be home till full moon."

²¹ With persuasive words she led him astray;
she seduced him with her smooth talk.
²² All at once he followed her
like an ox going to the slaughter,
like a deer stepping into a noose
²³ till an arrow pierces his liver,
like a bird darting into a snare,
little knowing it will cost him his life.

²⁴ Now then, my sons, listen to me;
pay attention to what I say.

²⁵ Do not let your heart turn to her ways
or stray into her paths.
²⁶ Many are the victims she has brought down;
her slain are a mighty throng.
²⁷ Her house is a highway to the grave,
leading down to the chambers of death.

Proverbs 8

¹ Does not wisdom call out?
Does not understanding raise her voice?
² On the heights along the way,
where the paths meet, she takes her stand;
³ beside the gates leading into the city,
at the entrances, she cries aloud:
⁴ "To you, O men, I call out;
I raise my voice to all mankind.
⁵ You who are simple, gain prudence;
you who are foolish, gain understanding.
⁶ Listen, for I have worthy things to say;
I open my lips to speak what is right.
⁷ My mouth speaks what is true,
for my lips detest wickedness.
⁸ All the words of my mouth are just;
none of them is crooked or perverse.
⁹ To the discerning all of them are right;
they are faultless to those who have knowledge.
¹⁰ Choose my instruction instead of silver,
knowledge rather than choice gold,
¹¹ for wisdom is more precious than rubies,
and nothing you desire can compare with her.

¹² "I, wisdom, dwell together with prudence;
I possess knowledge and discretion.
¹³ To fear the LORD is to hate evil;
I hate pride and arrogance,
evil behavior and perverse speech.
¹⁴ Counsel and sound judgment are mine;
I have understanding and power.

¹⁵ By me kings reign
and rulers make laws that are just;
¹⁶ by me princes govern,
and all nobles who rule on earth.
¹⁷ I love those who love me,
and those who seek me find me.
¹⁸ With me are riches and honor,
enduring wealth and prosperity.
¹⁹ My fruit is better than fine gold;
what I yield surpasses choice silver.
²⁰ I walk in the way of righteousness,
along the paths of justice,
²¹ bestowing wealth on those who love me
and making their treasuries full.

²² "The LORD brought me forth as the first of his works,
before his deeds of old;
²³ I was appointed from eternity,
from the beginning, before the world began.
²⁴ When there were no oceans, I was given birth,
when there were no springs abounding with water;
²⁵ before the mountains were settled in place,
before the hills, I was given birth,
²⁶ before he made the earth or its fields
or any of the dust of the world.
²⁷ I was there when he set the heavens in place,
when he marked out the horizon on the face of the deep,
²⁸ when he established the clouds above
and fixed securely the fountains of the deep,
²⁹ when he gave the sea its boundary
so the waters would not overstep his command,
and when he marked out the foundations of the earth.
³⁰ Then I was the craftsman at his side.
I was filled with delight day after day,
rejoicing always in his presence,
³¹ rejoicing in his whole world
and delighting in mankind.

[32] "Now then, my sons, listen to me;
blessed are those who keep my ways.
[33] Listen to my instruction and be wise;
do not ignore it.
[34] Blessed is the man who listens to me,
watching daily at my doors,
waiting at my doorway.
[35] For whoever finds me finds life
and receives favor from the LORD.
[36] But whoever fails to find me harms himself;
all who hate me love death."

Proverbs 9
[1] Wisdom has built her house;
she has hewn out its seven pillars.
[2] She has prepared her meat and mixed her wine;
she has also set her table.
[3] She has sent out her maids, and she calls
from the highest point of the city.
[4] "Let all who are simple come in here!"
she says to those who lack judgment.
[5] "Come, eat my food
and drink the wine I have mixed.
[6] Leave your simple ways and you will live;
walk in the way of understanding.

[7] "Whoever corrects a mocker invites insult;
whoever rebukes a wicked man incurs abuse.
[8] Do not rebuke a mocker or he will hate you;
rebuke a wise man and he will love you.
[9] Instruct a wise man and he will be wiser still;
teach a righteous man and he will add to his learning.

[10] "The fear of the LORD is the beginning of wisdom,
and knowledge of the Holy One is understanding.
[11] For through me your days will be many,
and years will be added to your life.
[12] If you are wise, your wisdom will reward you;
if you are a mocker, you alone will suffer."

¹³ The woman Folly is loud;
she is undisciplined and without knowledge.
¹⁴ She sits at the door of her house,
on a seat at the highest point of the city,
¹⁵ calling out to those who pass by,
who go straight on their way.
¹⁶ "Let all who are simple come in here!"
she says to those who lack judgment.
¹⁷ "Stolen water is sweet;
food eaten in secret is delicious!"
¹⁸ But little do they know that the dead are there,
that her guests are in the depths of the grave.

Proverbs 10

¹ The proverbs of Solomon:

A wise son brings joy to his father,
but a foolish son grief to his mother.

² Ill-gotten treasures are of no value,
but righteousness delivers from death.

³ The LORD does not let the righteous go hungry
but he thwarts the craving of the wicked.

⁴ Lazy hands make a man poor,
but diligent hands bring wealth.

⁵ He who gathers crops in summer is a wise son,
but he who sleeps during harvest is a disgraceful son.

⁶ Blessings crown the head of the righteous,
but violence overwhelms the mouth of the wicked.

⁷ The memory of the righteous will be a blessing,
but the name of the wicked will rot.

⁸ The wise in heart accept commands,
but a chattering fool comes to ruin.

⁹ The man of integrity walks securely,
but he who takes crooked paths will be found out.

¹⁰ He who winks maliciously causes grief,
and a chattering fool comes to ruin.

¹¹ The mouth of the righteous is a fountain of life,
but violence overwhelms the mouth of the wicked.

¹² Hatred stirs up dissension,
but love covers over all wrongs.

¹³ Wisdom is found on the lips of the discerning,
but a rod is for the back of him who lacks judgment.

¹⁴ Wise men store up knowledge,
but the mouth of a fool invites ruin.

¹⁵ The wealth of the rich is their fortified city,
but poverty is the ruin of the poor.

¹⁶ The wages of the righteous bring them life,
but the income of the wicked brings them punishment.

¹⁷ He who heeds discipline shows the way to life,
but whoever ignores correction leads others astray.

¹⁸ He who conceals his hatred has lying lips,
and whoever spreads slander is a fool.

¹⁹ When words are many, sin is not absent,
but he who holds his tongue is wise.

²⁰ The tongue of the righteous is choice silver,
but the heart of the wicked is of little value.

²¹ The lips of the righteous nourish many,
but fools die for lack of judgment.

[22] The blessing of the LORD brings wealth,
and he adds no trouble to it.

[23] A fool finds pleasure in evil conduct,
but a man of understanding delights in wisdom.

[24] What the wicked dreads will overtake him;
what the righteous desire will be granted.

[25] When the storm has swept by, the wicked are gone,
but the righteous stand firm forever.

[26] As vinegar to the teeth and smoke to the eyes,
so is a sluggard to those who send him.

[27] The fear of the LORD adds length to life,
but the years of the wicked are cut short.

[28] The prospect of the righteous is joy,
but the hopes of the wicked come to nothing.

[29] The way of the LORD is a refuge for the righteous,
but it is the ruin of those who do evil.

[30] The righteous will never be uprooted,
but the wicked will not remain in the land.

[31] The mouth of the righteous brings forth wisdom,
but a perverse tongue will be cut out.

[32] The lips of the righteous know what is fitting,
but the mouth of the wicked only what is perverse.

Proverbs 11

1 The LORD abhors dishonest scales,
but accurate weights are his delight.

2 When pride comes, then comes disgrace,
but with humility comes wisdom.

3 The integrity of the upright guides them,
but the unfaithful are destroyed by their duplicity.

4 Wealth is worthless in the day of wrath,
but righteousness delivers from death.

5 The righteousness of the blameless makes a straight way for them,
but the wicked are brought down by their own wickedness.

6 The righteousness of the upright delivers them,
but the unfaithful are trapped by evil desires.

7 When a wicked man dies, his hope perishes;
all he expected from his power comes to nothing.

8 The righteous man is rescued from trouble,
and it comes on the wicked instead.

9 With his mouth the godless destroys his neighbor,
but through knowledge the righteous escape.

10 When the righteous prosper, the city rejoices;
when the wicked perish, there are shouts of joy.

11 Through the blessing of the upright a city is exalted,
but by the mouth of the wicked it is destroyed.

12 A man who lacks judgment derides his neighbor,
but a man of understanding holds his tongue.

13 A gossip betrays a confidence,
but a trustworthy man keeps a secret.

¹⁴ For lack of guidance a nation falls,
but many advisers make victory sure.

¹⁵ He who puts up security for another will surely suffer,
but whoever refuses to strike hands in pledge is safe.

¹⁶ A kindhearted woman gains respect,
but ruthless men gain only wealth.

¹⁷ A kind man benefits himself,
but a cruel man brings trouble on himself.

¹⁸ The wicked man earns deceptive wages,
but he who sows righteousness reaps a sure reward.

¹⁹ The truly righteous man attains life,
but he who pursues evil goes to his death.

²⁰ The LORD detests men of perverse heart
but he delights in those whose ways are blameless.

²¹ Be sure of this: The wicked will not go unpunished,
but those who are righteous will go free.

²² Like a gold ring in a pig's snout
is a beautiful woman who shows no discretion.

²³ The desire of the righteous ends only in good,
but the hope of the wicked only in wrath.

²⁴ One man gives freely, yet gains even more;
another withholds unduly, but comes to poverty.

²⁵ A generous man will prosper;
he who refreshes others will himself be refreshed.

²⁶ People curse the man who hoards grain,
but blessing crowns him who is willing to sell.

²⁷ He who seeks good finds goodwill,
but evil comes to him who searches for it.

²⁸ Whoever trusts in his riches will fall,
but the righteous will thrive like a green leaf.

²⁹ He who brings trouble on his family will inherit only wind,
and the fool will be servant to the wise.

³⁰ The fruit of the righteous is a tree of life,
and he who wins souls is wise.

³¹ If the righteous receive their due on earth,
how much more the ungodly and the sinner!

Proverbs 12

¹ Whoever loves discipline loves knowledge,
but he who hates correction is stupid.

² A good man obtains favor from the LORD,
but the LORD condemns a crafty man.

³ A man cannot be established through wickedness,
but the righteous cannot be uprooted.

⁴ A wife of noble character is her husband's crown,
but a disgraceful wife is like decay in his bones.

⁵ The plans of the righteous are just,
but the advice of the wicked is deceitful.

⁶ The words of the wicked lie in wait for blood,
but the speech of the upright rescues them.

⁷ Wicked men are overthrown and are no more,
but the house of the righteous stands firm.

⁸ A man is praised according to his wisdom,
but men with warped minds are despised.

⁹ Better to be a nobody and yet have a servant
than pretend to be somebody and have no food.

¹⁰ A righteous man cares for the needs of his animal,
but the kindest acts of the wicked are cruel.

¹¹ He who works his land will have abundant food,
but he who chases fantasies lacks judgment.

¹² The wicked desire the plunder of evil men,
but the root of the righteous flourishes.

¹³ An evil man is trapped by his sinful talk,
but a righteous man escapes trouble.

¹⁴ From the fruit of his lips a man is filled with good things
as surely as the work of his hands rewards him.

¹⁵ The way of a fool seems right to him,
but a wise man listens to advice.

¹⁶ A fool shows his annoyance at once,
but a prudent man overlooks an insult.

¹⁷ A truthful witness gives honest testimony,
but a false witness tells lies.

¹⁸ Reckless words pierce like a sword,
but the tongue of the wise brings healing.

¹⁹ Truthful lips endure forever,
but a lying tongue lasts only a moment.

²⁰ There is deceit in the hearts of those who plot evil,
but joy for those who promote peace.

²¹ No harm befalls the righteous,
but the wicked have their fill of trouble.

[22] The LORD detests lying lips,
but he delights in men who are truthful.

[23] A prudent man keeps his knowledge to himself,
but the heart of fools blurts out folly.

[24] Diligent hands will rule,
but laziness ends in slave labor.

[25] An anxious heart weighs a man down,
but a kind word cheers him up.

[26] A righteous man is cautious in friendship,
but the way of the wicked leads them astray.

[27] The lazy man does not roast his game,
but the diligent man prizes his possessions.

[28] In the way of righteousness there is life;
along that path is immortality.

Proverbs 13

[1] A wise son heeds his father's instruction,
but a mocker does not listen to rebuke.

[2] From the fruit of his lips a man enjoys good things,
but the unfaithful have a craving for violence.

[3] He who guards his lips guards his life,
but he who speaks rashly will come to ruin.

[4] The sluggard craves and gets nothing,
but the desires of the diligent are fully satisfied.

[5] The righteous hate what is false,
but the wicked bring shame and disgrace.

[6] Righteousness guards the man of integrity,
but wickedness overthrows the sinner.

⁷ One man pretends to be rich, yet has nothing;
another pretends to be poor, yet has great wealth.

⁸ A man's riches may ransom his life,
but a poor man hears no threat.

⁹ The light of the righteous shines brightly,
but the lamp of the wicked is snuffed out.

¹⁰ Pride only breeds quarrels,
but wisdom is found in those who take advice.

¹¹ Dishonest money dwindles away,
but he who gathers money little by little makes it grow.

¹² Hope deferred makes the heart sick,
but a longing fulfilled is a tree of life.

¹³ He who scorns instruction will pay for it,
but he who respects a command is rewarded.

¹⁴ The teaching of the wise is a fountain of life,
turning a man from the snares of death.

¹⁵ Good understanding wins favor,
but the way of the unfaithful is hard.

¹⁶ Every prudent man acts out of knowledge,
but a fool exposes his folly.

¹⁷ A wicked messenger falls into trouble,
but a trustworthy envoy brings healing.

¹⁸ He who ignores discipline comes to poverty and shame,
but whoever heeds correction is honored.

¹⁹ A longing fulfilled is sweet to the soul,
but fools detest turning from evil.

[20] He who walks with the wise grows wise,
but a companion of fools suffers harm.

[21] Misfortune pursues the sinner,
but prosperity is the reward of the righteous.

[22] A good man leaves an inheritance for his children's children,
but a sinner's wealth is stored up for the righteous.

[23] A poor man's field may produce abundant food,
but injustice sweeps it away.

[24] He who spares the rod hates his son,
but he who loves him is careful to discipline him.

[25] The righteous eat to their hearts' content,
but the stomach of the wicked goes hungry.

Proverbs 14
[1] The wise woman builds her house,
but with her own hands the foolish one tears hers down.

[2] He whose walk is upright fears the LORD,
but he whose ways are devious despises him.

[3] A fool's talk brings a rod to his back,
but the lips of the wise protect them.

[4] Where there are no oxen, the manger is empty,
but from the strength of an ox comes an abundant harvest.

[5] A truthful witness does not deceive,
but a false witness pours out lies.

[6] The mocker seeks wisdom and finds none,
but knowledge comes easily to the discerning.

[7] Stay away from a foolish man,
for you will not find knowledge on his lips.

⁸ The wisdom of the prudent is to give thought to their ways,
but the folly of fools is deception.

⁹ Fools mock at making amends for sin,
but goodwill is found among the upright.

¹⁰ Each heart knows its own bitterness,
and no one else can share its joy.

¹¹ The house of the wicked will be destroyed,
but the tent of the upright will flourish.

¹² There is a way that seems right to a man,
but in the end it leads to death.

¹³ Even in laughter the heart may ache,
and joy may end in grief.

¹⁴ The faithless will be fully repaid for their ways,
and the good man rewarded for his.

¹⁵ A simple man believes anything,
but a prudent man gives thought to his steps.

¹⁶ A wise man fears the LORD and shuns evil,
but a fool is hotheaded and reckless.

¹⁷ A quick-tempered man does foolish things,
and a crafty man is hated.

¹⁸ The simple inherit folly,
but the prudent are crowned with knowledge.

¹⁹ Evil men will bow down in the presence of the good,
and the wicked at the gates of the righteous.

²⁰ The poor are shunned even by their neighbors,
but the rich have many friends.

²¹ He who despises his neighbor sins,
but blessed is he who is kind to the needy.

²² Do not those who plot evil go astray?
But those who plan what is good find love and faithfulness.

²³ All hard work brings a profit,
but mere talk leads only to poverty.

²⁴ The wealth of the wise is their crown,
but the folly of fools yields folly.

²⁵ A truthful witness saves lives,
but a false witness is deceitful.

²⁶ He who fears the LORD has a secure fortress,
and for his children it will be a refuge.

²⁷ The fear of the LORD is a fountain of life,
turning a man from the snares of death.

²⁸ A large population is a king's glory,
but without subjects a prince is ruined.

²⁹ A patient man has great understanding,
but a quick-tempered man displays folly.

³⁰ A heart at peace gives life to the body,
but envy rots the bones.

³¹ He who oppresses the poor shows contempt for their Maker,
but whoever is kind to the needy honors God.

³² When calamity comes, the wicked are brought down,
but even in death the righteous have a refuge.

³³ Wisdom reposes in the heart of the discerning
and even among fools she lets herself be known.

³⁴ Righteousness exalts a nation,
but sin is a disgrace to any people.

³⁵ A king delights in a wise servant,
but a shameful servant incurs his wrath.

Proverbs 15

¹ A gentle answer turns away wrath,
but a harsh word stirs up anger.

² The tongue of the wise commends knowledge,
but the mouth of the fool gushes folly.

³ The eyes of the LORD are everywhere,
keeping watch on the wicked and the good.

⁴ The tongue that brings healing is a tree of life,
but a deceitful tongue crushes the spirit.

⁵ A fool spurns his father's discipline,
but whoever heeds correction shows prudence.

⁶ The house of the righteous contains great treasure,
but the income of the wicked brings them trouble.

⁷ The lips of the wise spread knowledge;
not so the hearts of fools.

⁸ The LORD detests the sacrifice of the wicked,
but the prayer of the upright pleases him.

⁹ The LORD detests the way of the wicked
but he loves those who pursue righteousness.

¹⁰ Stern discipline awaits him who leaves the path;
he who hates correction will die.

¹¹ Death and Destruction lie open before the LORD—
how much more the hearts of men!

¹² A mocker resents correction;
he will not consult the wise.

¹³ A happy heart makes the face cheerful,
but heartache crushes the spirit.

¹⁴ The discerning heart seeks knowledge,
but the mouth of a fool feeds on folly.

¹⁵ All the days of the oppressed are wretched,
but the cheerful heart has a continual feast.

¹⁶ Better a little with the fear of the LORD
than great wealth with turmoil.

¹⁷ Better a meal of vegetables where there is love
than a fattened calf with hatred.

¹⁸ A hot-tempered man stirs up dissension,
but a patient man calms a quarrel.

¹⁹ The way of the sluggard is blocked with thorns,
but the path of the upright is a highway.

²⁰ A wise son brings joy to his father,
but a foolish man despises his mother.

²¹ Folly delights a man who lacks judgment,
but a man of understanding keeps a straight course.

²² Plans fail for lack of counsel,
but with many advisers they succeed.

²³ A man finds joy in giving an apt reply-
and how good is a timely word!

²⁴ The path of life leads upward for the wise
to keep him from going down to the grave.

²⁵ The LORD tears down the proud man's house
but he keeps the widow's boundaries intact.

²⁶ The LORD detests the thoughts of the wicked,
but those of the pure are pleasing to him.

²⁷ A greedy man brings trouble to his family,
but he who hates bribes will live.

²⁸ The heart of the righteous weighs its answers,
but the mouth of the wicked gushes evil.

²⁹ The LORD is far from the wicked
but he hears the prayer of the righteous.

³⁰ A cheerful look brings joy to the heart,
and good news gives health to the bones.

³¹ He who listens to a life-giving rebuke
will be at home among the wise.

³² He who ignores discipline despises himself,
but whoever heeds correction gains understanding.

³³ The fear of the LORD teaches a man wisdom,
and humility comes before honor.

Proverbs 16

¹ To man belong the plans of the heart,
but from the LORD comes the reply of the tongue.

² All a man's ways seem innocent to him,
but motives are weighed by the LORD.

³ Commit to the LORD whatever you do,
and your plans will succeed.

⁴ The LORD works out everything for his own ends-
even the wicked for a day of disaster.

⁵ The LORD detests all the proud of heart.
Be sure of this: They will not go unpunished.

⁶ Through love and faithfulness sin is atoned for;
through the fear of the LORD a man avoids evil.

⁷ When a man's ways are pleasing to the LORD,
he makes even his enemies live at peace with him.

⁸ Better a little with righteousness
than much gain with injustice.

⁹ In his heart a man plans his course,
but the LORD determines his steps.

¹⁰ The lips of a king speak as an oracle,
and his mouth should not betray justice.

¹¹ Honest scales and balances are from the LORD;
all the weights in the bag are of his making.

¹² Kings detest wrongdoing,
for a throne is established through righteousness.

¹³ Kings take pleasure in honest lips;
they value a man who speaks the truth.

¹⁴ A king's wrath is a messenger of death,
but a wise man will appease it.

¹⁵ When a king's face brightens, it means life;
his favor is like a rain cloud in spring.

¹⁶ How much better to get wisdom than gold,
to choose understanding rather than silver!

¹⁷ The highway of the upright avoids evil;
he who guards his way guards his life.

[18] Pride goes before destruction,
a haughty spirit before a fall.

[19] Better to be lowly in spirit and among the oppressed
than to share plunder with the proud.

[20] Whoever gives heed to instruction prospers,
and blessed is he who trusts in the LORD.

[21] The wise in heart are called discerning,
and pleasant words promote instruction.

[22] Understanding is a fountain of life to those who have it,
but folly brings punishment to fools.

[23] A wise man's heart guides his mouth,
and his lips promote instruction.

[24] Pleasant words are a honeycomb,
sweet to the soul and healing to the bones.

[25] There is a way that seems right to a man,
but in the end it leads to death.

[26] The laborer's appetite works for him;
his hunger drives him on.

[27] A scoundrel plots evil,
and his speech is like a scorching fire.

[28] A perverse man stirs up dissension,
and a gossip separates close friends.

[29] A violent man entices his neighbor
and leads him down a path that is not good.

[30] He who winks with his eye is plotting perversity;
he who purses his lips is bent on evil.

³¹ Gray hair is a crown of splendor;
it is attained by a righteous life.

³² Better a patient man than a warrior,
a man who controls his temper than one who takes a city.

³³ The lot is cast into the lap,
but its every decision is from the LORD.

Proverbs 17

¹ Better a dry crust with peace and quiet
than a house full of feasting, with strife.

² A wise servant will rule over a disgraceful son,
and will share the inheritance as one of the brothers.

³ The crucible for silver and the furnace for gold,
but the LORD tests the heart.

⁴ A wicked man listens to evil lips;
a liar pays attention to a malicious tongue.

⁵ He who mocks the poor shows contempt for their Maker;
whoever gloats over disaster will not go unpunished.

⁶ Children's children are a crown to the aged,
and parents are the pride of their children.

⁷ Arrogant lips are unsuited to a fool-
how much worse lying lips to a ruler!

⁸ A bribe is a charm to the one who gives it;
wherever he turns, he succeeds.

⁹ He who covers over an offense promotes love,
but whoever repeats the matter separates close friends.

¹⁰ A rebuke impresses a man of discernment
more than a hundred lashes a fool.

¹¹ An evil man is bent only on rebellion;
a merciless official will be sent against him.

¹² Better to meet a bear robbed of her cubs
than a fool in his folly.

¹³ If a man pays back evil for good,
evil will never leave his house.

¹⁴ Starting a quarrel is like breaching a dam;
so drop the matter before a dispute breaks out.

¹⁵ Acquitting the guilty and condemning the innocent-
the LORD detests them both.

¹⁶ Of what use is money in the hand of a fool,
since he has no desire to get wisdom?

¹⁷ A friend loves at all times,
and a brother is born for adversity.

¹⁸ A man lacking in judgment strikes hands in pledge
and puts up security for his neighbor.

¹⁹ He who loves a quarrel loves sin;
he who builds a high gate invites destruction.

²⁰ A man of perverse heart does not prosper;
he whose tongue is deceitful falls into trouble.

²¹ To have a fool for a son brings grief;
there is no joy for the father of a fool.

²² A cheerful heart is good medicine,
but a crushed spirit dries up the bones.

²³ A wicked man accepts a bribe in secret
to pervert the course of justice.

^{24} A discerning man keeps wisdom in view,
but a fool's eyes wander to the ends of the earth.

^{25} A foolish son brings grief to his father
and bitterness to the one who bore him.

^{26} It is not good to punish an innocent man,
or to flog officials for their integrity.

^{27} A man of knowledge uses words with restraint,
and a man of understanding is even-tempered.

^{28} Even a fool is thought wise if he keeps silent,
and discerning if he holds his tongue.

Proverbs 18

^{1} An unfriendly man pursues selfish ends;
he defies all sound judgment.

^{2} A fool finds no pleasure in understanding
but delights in airing his own opinions.

^{3} When wickedness comes, so does contempt,
and with shame comes disgrace.

^{4} The words of a man's mouth are deep waters,
but the fountain of wisdom is a bubbling brook.

^{5} It is not good to be partial to the wicked
or to deprive the innocent of justice.

^{6} A fool's lips bring him strife,
and his mouth invites a beating.

^{7} A fool's mouth is his undoing,
and his lips are a snare to his soul.

^{8} The words of a gossip are like choice morsels;
they go down to a man's inmost parts.

⁹ One who is slack in his work
is brother to one who destroys.

¹⁰ The name of the LORD is a strong tower;
the righteous run to it and are safe.

¹¹ The wealth of the rich is their fortified city;
they imagine it an unscalable wall.

¹² Before his downfall a man's heart is proud,
but humility comes before honor.

¹³ He who answers before listening-
that is his folly and his shame.

¹⁴ A man's spirit sustains him in sickness,
but a crushed spirit who can bear?

¹⁵ The heart of the discerning acquires knowledge;
the ears of the wise seek it out.

¹⁶ A gift opens the way for the giver
and ushers him into the presence of the great.

¹⁷ The first to present his case seems right,
till another comes forward and questions him.

¹⁸ Casting the lot settles disputes
and keeps strong opponents apart.

¹⁹ An offended brother is more unyielding than a fortified city,
and disputes are like the barred gates of a citadel.

²⁰ From the fruit of his mouth a man's stomach is filled;
with the harvest from his lips he is satisfied.

²¹ The tongue has the power of life and death,
and those who love it will eat its fruit.

²² He who finds a wife finds what is good
and receives favor from the LORD.

²³ A poor man pleads for mercy,
but a rich man answers harshly.

²⁴ A man of many companions may come to ruin,
but there is a friend who sticks closer than a brother.

Proverbs 19
¹ Better a poor man whose walk is blameless
than a fool whose lips are perverse.

² It is not good to have zeal without knowledge,
nor to be hasty and miss the way.

³ A man's own folly ruins his life,
yet his heart rages against the LORD.

⁴ Wealth brings many friends,
but a poor man's friend deserts him.

⁵ A false witness will not go unpunished,
and he who pours out lies will not go free.

⁶ Many curry favor with a ruler,
and everyone is the friend of a man who gives gifts.

⁷ A poor man is shunned by all his relatives-
how much more do his friends avoid him!
Though he pursues them with pleading,
they are nowhere to be found.

⁸ He who gets wisdom loves his own soul;
he who cherishes understanding prospers.

⁹ A false witness will not go unpunished,
and he who pours out lies will perish.

[10] It is not fitting for a fool to live in luxury-
how much worse for a slave to rule over princes!

[11] A man's wisdom gives him patience;
it is to his glory to overlook an offense.

[12] A king's rage is like the roar of a lion,
but his favor is like dew on the grass.

[13] A foolish son is his father's ruin,
and a quarrelsome wife is like a constant dripping.

[14] Houses and wealth are inherited from parents,
but a prudent wife is from the LORD.

[15] Laziness brings on deep sleep,
and the shiftless man goes hungry.

[16] He who obeys instructions guards his life,
but he who is contemptuous of his ways will die.

[17] He who is kind to the poor lends to the LORD,
and he will reward him for what he has done.

[18] Discipline your son, for in that there is hope;
do not be a willing party to his death.

[19] A hot-tempered man must pay the penalty;
if you rescue him, you will have to do it again.

[20] Listen to advice and accept instruction,
and in the end you will be wise.

[21] Many are the plans in a man's heart,
but it is the LORD's purpose that prevails.

[22] What a man desires is unfailing love;
better to be poor than a liar.

²³ The fear of the LORD leads to life:
Then one rests content, untouched by trouble.

²⁴ The sluggard buries his hand in the dish;
he will not even bring it back to his mouth!

²⁵ Flog a mocker, and the simple will learn prudence;
rebuke a discerning man, and he will gain knowledge.

²⁶ He who robs his father and drives out his mother
is a son who brings shame and disgrace.

²⁷ Stop listening to instruction, my son,
and you will stray from the words of knowledge.

²⁸ A corrupt witness mocks at justice,
and the mouth of the wicked gulps down evil.

²⁹ Penalties are prepared for mockers,
and beatings for the backs of fools.

Proverbs 20

¹ Wine is a mocker and beer a brawler;
whoever is led astray by them is not wise.

² A king's wrath is like the roar of a lion;
he who angers him forfeits his life.

³ It is to a man's honor to avoid strife,
but every fool is quick to quarrel.

⁴ A sluggard does not plow in season;
so at harvest time he looks but finds nothing.

⁵ The purposes of a man's heart are deep waters,
but a man of understanding draws them out.

⁶ Many a man claims to have unfailing love,
but a faithful man who can find?

[7] The righteous man leads a blameless life;
blessed are his children after him.

[8] When a king sits on his throne to judge,
he winnows out all evil with his eyes.

[9] Who can say, "I have kept my heart pure;
I am clean and without sin"?

[10] Differing weights and differing measures-
the LORD detests them both.

[11] Even a child is known by his actions,
by whether his conduct is pure and right.

[12] Ears that hear and eyes that see-
the LORD has made them both.

[13] Do not love sleep or you will grow poor;
stay awake and you will have food to spare.

[14] "It's no good, it's no good!" says the buyer;
then off he goes and boasts about his purchase.

[15] Gold there is, and rubies in abundance,
but lips that speak knowledge are a rare jewel.

[16] Take the garment of one who puts up security for a stranger;
hold it in pledge if he does it for a wayward woman.

[17] Food gained by fraud tastes sweet to a man,
but he ends up with a mouth full of gravel.

[18] Make plans by seeking advice;
if you wage war, obtain guidance.

[19] A gossip betrays a confidence;
so avoid a man who talks too much.

²⁰ If a man curses his father or mother,
his lamp will be snuffed out in pitch darkness.

²¹ An inheritance quickly gained at the beginning
will not be blessed at the end.

²² Do not say, "I'll pay you back for this wrong!"
Wait for the LORD , and he will deliver you.

²³ The LORD detests differing weights,
and dishonest scales do not please him.

²⁴ A man's steps are directed by the LORD.
How then can anyone understand his own way?

²⁵ It is a trap for a man to dedicate something rashly
and only later to consider his vows.

²⁶ A wise king winnows out the wicked;
he drives the threshing wheel over them.

²⁷ The lamp of the LORD searches the spirit of a man;
it searches out his inmost being.

²⁸ Love and faithfulness keep a king safe;
through love his throne is made secure.

²⁹ The glory of young men is their strength,
gray hair the splendor of the old.

³⁰ Blows and wounds cleanse away evil,
and beatings purge the inmost being.

Proverbs 21

¹ The king's heart is in the hand of the LORD;
he directs it like a watercourse wherever he pleases.

² All a man's ways seem right to him,
but the LORD weighs the heart.

³ To do what is right and just
is more acceptable to the LORD than sacrifice.

⁴ Haughty eyes and a proud heart,
the lamp of the wicked, are sin!

⁵ The plans of the diligent lead to profit
as surely as haste leads to poverty.

⁶ A fortune made by a lying tongue
is a fleeting vapor and a deadly snare.

⁷ The violence of the wicked will drag them away,
for they refuse to do what is right.

⁸ The way of the guilty is devious,
but the conduct of the innocent is upright.

⁹ Better to live on a corner of the roof
than share a house with a quarrelsome wife.

¹⁰ The wicked man craves evil;
his neighbor gets no mercy from him.

¹¹ When a mocker is punished, the simple gain wisdom;
when a wise man is instructed, he gets knowledge.

¹² The Righteous One takes note of the house of the wicked
and brings the wicked to ruin.

¹³ If a man shuts his ears to the cry of the poor,
he too will cry out and not be answered.

¹⁴ A gift given in secret soothes anger,
and a bribe concealed in the cloak pacifies great wrath.

¹⁵ When justice is done, it brings joy to the righteous
but terror to evildoers.

¹⁶ A man who strays from the path of understanding
comes to rest in the company of the dead.

¹⁷ He who loves pleasure will become poor;
whoever loves wine and oil will never be rich.

¹⁸ The wicked become a ransom for the righteous,
and the unfaithful for the upright.

¹⁹ Better to live in a desert
than with a quarrelsome and ill-tempered wife.

²⁰ In the house of the wise are stores of choice food and oil,
but a foolish man devours all he has.

²¹ He who pursues righteousness and love
finds life, prosperity and honor.

²² A wise man attacks the city of the mighty
and pulls down the stronghold in which they trust.

²³ He who guards his mouth and his tongue
keeps himself from calamity.

²⁴ The proud and arrogant man-"Mocker" is his name;
he behaves with overweening pride.

²⁵ The sluggard's craving will be the death of him,
because his hands refuse to work.
²⁶ All day long he craves for more,
but the righteous give without sparing.

²⁷ The sacrifice of the wicked is detestable-
how much more so when brought with evil intent!

²⁸ A false witness will perish,
and whoever listens to him will be destroyed forever.

²⁹ A wicked man puts up a bold front,
but an upright man gives thought to his ways.

³⁰ There is no wisdom, no insight, no plan
that can succeed against the LORD.

³¹ The horse is made ready for the day of battle,
but victory rests with the LORD.

Proverbs 22

¹ A good name is more desirable than great riches;
to be esteemed is better than silver or gold.

² Rich and poor have this in common:
The LORD is the Maker of them all.

³ A prudent man sees danger and takes refuge,
but the simple keep going and suffer for it.

⁴ Humility and the fear of the LORD
bring wealth and honor and life.

⁵ In the paths of the wicked lie thorns and snares,
but he who guards his soul stays far from them.

⁶ Train a child in the way he should go,
and when he is old he will not turn from it.

⁷ The rich rule over the poor,
and the borrower is servant to the lender.

⁸ He who sows wickedness reaps trouble,
and the rod of his fury will be destroyed.

⁹ A generous man will himself be blessed,
for he shares his food with the poor.

¹⁰ Drive out the mocker, and out goes strife;
quarrels and insults are ended.

¹¹ He who loves a pure heart and whose speech is gracious
will have the king for his friend.

¹² The eyes of the LORD keep watch over knowledge,
but he frustrates the words of the unfaithful.

¹³ The sluggard says, "There is a lion outside!"
or, "I will be murdered in the streets!"

¹⁴ The mouth of an adulteress is a deep pit;
he who is under the LORD's wrath will fall into it.

¹⁵ Folly is bound up in the heart of a child,
but the rod of discipline will drive it far from him.

¹⁶ He who oppresses the poor to increase his wealth
and he who gives gifts to the rich-both come to poverty.

¹⁷ Pay attention and listen to the sayings of the wise;
apply your heart to what I teach,
¹⁸ for it is pleasing when you keep them in your heart
and have all of them ready on your lips.
¹⁹ So that your trust may be in the LORD,
I teach you today, even you.
²⁰ Have I not written thirty sayings for you,
sayings of counsel and knowledge,
²¹ teaching you true and reliable words,
so that you can give sound answers
to him who sent you?

²² Do not exploit the poor because they are poor
and do not crush the needy in court,

²³ for the LORD will take up their case
and will plunder those who plunder them.

²⁴ Do not make friends with a hot-tempered man,
do not associate with one easily angered,
²⁵ or you may learn his ways
and get yourself ensnared.

²⁶ Do not be a man who strikes hands in pledge
or puts up security for debts;
²⁷ if you lack the means to pay,
your very bed will be snatched from under you.

²⁸ Do not move an ancient boundary stone
set up by your forefathers.

²⁹ Do you see a man skilled in his work?
He will serve before kings;
he will not serve before obscure men.

Proverbs 23
¹ When you sit to dine with a ruler,
note well what is before you,
² and put a knife to your throat
if you are given to gluttony.
³ Do not crave his delicacies,
for that food is deceptive.

⁴ Do not wear yourself out to get rich;
have the wisdom to show restraint.
⁵ Cast but a glance at riches, and they are gone,
for they will surely sprout wings
and fly off to the sky like an eagle.

⁶ Do not eat the food of a stingy man,
do not crave his delicacies;

7 for he is the kind of man
who is always thinking about the cost.
"Eat and drink," he says to you,
but his heart is not with you.
8 You will vomit up the little you have eaten
and will have wasted your compliments.

9 Do not speak to a fool,
for he will scorn the wisdom of your words.

10 Do not move an ancient boundary stone
or encroach on the fields of the fatherless,
11 for their Defender is strong;
he will take up their case against you.

12 Apply your heart to instruction
and your ears to words of knowledge.

13 Do not withhold discipline from a child;
if you punish him with the rod, he will not die.
14 Punish him with the rod
and save his soul from death.

15 My son, if your heart is wise,
then my heart will be glad;
16 my inmost being will rejoice
when your lips speak what is right.

17 Do not let your heart envy sinners,
but always be zealous for the fear of the LORD.
18 There is surely a future hope for you,
and your hope will not be cut off.

19 Listen, my son, and be wise,
and keep your heart on the right path.
20 Do not join those who drink too much wine
or gorge themselves on meat,
21 for drunkards and gluttons become poor,
and drowsiness clothes them in rags.

²² Listen to your father, who gave you life,
and do not despise your mother when she is old.
²³ Buy the truth and do not sell it;
get wisdom, discipline and understanding.
²⁴ The father of a righteous man has great joy;
he who has a wise son delights in him.
²⁵ May your father and mother be glad;
may she who gave you birth rejoice!
²⁶ My son, give me your heart
and let your eyes keep to my ways,
²⁷ for a prostitute is a deep pit
and a wayward wife is a narrow well.
²⁸ Like a bandit she lies in wait,
and multiplies the unfaithful among men.

²⁹ Who has woe? Who has sorrow?
Who has strife? Who has complaints?
Who has needless bruises? Who has bloodshot eyes?
³⁰ Those who linger over wine,
who go to sample bowls of mixed wine.
³¹ Do not gaze at wine when it is red,
when it sparkles in the cup,
when it goes down smoothly!
³² In the end it bites like a snake
and poisons like a viper.
³³ Your eyes will see strange sights
and your mind imagine confusing things.
³⁴ You will be like one sleeping on the high seas,
lying on top of the rigging.
³⁵ "They hit me," you will say, "but I'm not hurt!
They beat me, but I don't feel it!
When will I wake up
so I can find another drink?"

Proverbs 24

[1] Do not envy wicked men,
do not desire their company;
[2] for their hearts plot violence,
and their lips talk about making trouble.

[3] By wisdom a house is built,
and through understanding it is established;
[4] through knowledge its rooms are filled
with rare and beautiful treasures.

[5] A wise man has great power,
and a man of knowledge increases strength;
[6] for waging war you need guidance,
and for victory many advisers.

[7] Wisdom is too high for a fool;
in the assembly at the gate he has nothing to say.

[8] He who plots evil
will be known as a schemer.
[9] The schemes of folly are sin,
and men detest a mocker.

[10] If you falter in times of trouble,
how small is your strength!

[11] Rescue those being led away to death;
hold back those staggering toward slaughter.
[12] If you say, "But we knew nothing about this,"
does not he who weighs the heart perceive it?
Does not he who guards your life know it?
Will he not repay each person according to what he has done?

[13] Eat honey, my son, for it is good;
honey from the comb is sweet to your taste.
[14] Know also that wisdom is sweet to your soul;
if you find it, there is a future hope for you,
and your hope will not be cut off.

[15] Do not lie in wait like an outlaw against a righteous man's house,
do not raid his dwelling place;
[16] for though a righteous man falls seven times, he rises again,
but the wicked are brought down by calamity.

[17] Do not gloat when your enemy falls;
when he stumbles, do not let your heart rejoice,
[18] or the LORD will see and disapprove
and turn his wrath away from him.

[19] Do not fret because of evil men
or be envious of the wicked,
[20] for the evil man has no future hope,
and the lamp of the wicked will be snuffed out.

[21] Fear the LORD and the king, my son,
and do not join with the rebellious,
[22] for those two will send sudden destruction upon them,
and who knows what calamities they can bring?

[23] These also are sayings of the wise:

To show partiality in judging is not good:
[24] Whoever says to the guilty, "You are innocent"-
peoples will curse him and nations denounce him.
[25] But it will go well with those who convict the guilty,
and rich blessing will come upon them.

[26] An honest answer
is like a kiss on the lips.

[27] Finish your outdoor work
and get your fields ready;
after that, build your house.

[28] Do not testify against your neighbor without cause,
or use your lips to deceive.
[29] Do not say, "I'll do to him as he has done to me;
I'll pay that man back for what he did."

³⁰ I went past the field of the sluggard,
past the vineyard of the man who lacks judgment;
³¹ thorns had come up everywhere,
the ground was covered with weeds,
and the stone wall was in ruins.
³² I applied my heart to what I observed
and learned a lesson from what I saw:
³³ A little sleep, a little slumber,
a little folding of the hands to rest-
³⁴ and poverty will come on you like a bandit
and scarcity like an armed man.

Proverbs 25

¹ These are more proverbs of Solomon, copied by the men of Hezekiah
king of Judah:

² It is the glory of God to conceal a matter;
to search out a matter is the glory of kings.

³ As the heavens are high and the earth is deep,
so the hearts of kings are unsearchable.

⁴ Remove the dross from the silver,
and out comes material for the silversmith;
⁵ remove the wicked from the king's presence,
and his throne will be established through righteousness.

⁶ Do not exalt yourself in the king's presence,
and do not claim a place among great men;
⁷ it is better for him to say to you, "Come up here,"
than for him to humiliate you before a nobleman.

What you have seen with your eyes
⁸ do not bring hastily to court,
for what will you do in the end
if your neighbor puts you to shame?

⁹ If you argue your case with a neighbor,
do not betray another man's confidence,

¹⁰ or he who hears it may shame you
and you will never lose your bad reputation.

¹¹ A word aptly spoken
is like apples of gold in settings of silver.

¹² Like an earring of gold or an ornament of fine gold
is a wise man's rebuke to a listening ear.

¹³ Like the coolness of snow at harvest time
is a trustworthy messenger to those who send him;
he refreshes the spirit of his masters.

¹⁴ Like clouds and wind without rain
is a man who boasts of gifts he does not give.

¹⁵ Through patience a ruler can be persuaded,
and a gentle tongue can break a bone.

¹⁶ If you find honey, eat just enough-
too much of it, and you will vomit.
¹⁷ Seldom set foot in your neighbor's house-
too much of you, and he will hate you.

¹⁸ Like a club or a sword or a sharp arrow
is the man who gives false testimony against his neighbor.

¹⁹ Like a bad tooth or a lame foot
is reliance on the unfaithful in times of trouble.

²⁰ Like one who takes away a garment on a cold day,
or like vinegar poured on soda,
is one who sings songs to a heavy heart.

²¹ If your enemy is hungry, give him food to eat;
if he is thirsty, give him water to drink.
²² In doing this, you will heap burning coals on his head,
and the LORD will reward you.

²³ As a north wind brings rain,
so a sly tongue brings angry looks.

²⁴ Better to live on a corner of the roof
than share a house with a quarrelsome wife.

²⁵ Like cold water to a weary soul
is good news from a distant land.

²⁶ Like a muddied spring or a polluted well
is a righteous man who gives way to the wicked.

²⁷ It is not good to eat too much honey,
nor is it honorable to seek one's own honor.

²⁸ Like a city whose walls are broken down
is a man who lacks self-control.

Proverbs 26

¹ Like snow in summer or rain in harvest,
honor is not fitting for a fool.

² Like a fluttering sparrow or a darting swallow,
an undeserved curse does not come to rest.

³ A whip for the horse, a halter for the donkey,
and a rod for the backs of fools!

⁴ Do not answer a fool according to his folly,
or you will be like him yourself.

⁵ Answer a fool according to his folly,
or he will be wise in his own eyes.

⁶ Like cutting off one's feet or drinking violence
is the sending of a message by the hand of a fool.

⁷ Like a lame man's legs that hang limp
is a proverb in the mouth of a fool.

⁸ Like tying a stone in a sling
is the giving of honor to a fool.

⁹ Like a thornbush in a drunkard's hand
is a proverb in the mouth of a fool.

¹⁰ Like an archer who wounds at random
is he who hires a fool or any passer-by.

¹¹ As a dog returns to its vomit,
so a fool repeats his folly.

¹² Do you see a man wise in his own eyes?
There is more hope for a fool than for him.

¹³ The sluggard says, "There is a lion in the road,
a fierce lion roaming the streets!"

¹⁴ As a door turns on its hinges,
so a sluggard turns on his bed.

¹⁵ The sluggard buries his hand in the dish;
he is too lazy to bring it back to his mouth.

¹⁶ The sluggard is wiser in his own eyes
than seven men who answer discreetly.

¹⁷ Like one who seizes a dog by the ears
is a passer-by who meddles in a quarrel not his own.

¹⁸ Like a madman shooting
firebrands or deadly arrows
¹⁹ is a man who deceives his neighbor
and says, "I was only joking!"

²⁰ Without wood a fire goes out;
without gossip a quarrel dies down.

²¹ As charcoal to embers and as wood to fire,
so is a quarrelsome man for kindling strife.

²² The words of a gossip are like choice morsels;
they go down to a man's inmost parts.

²³ Like a coating of glaze over earthenware
are fervent lips with an evil heart.

²⁴ A malicious man disguises himself with his lips,
but in his heart he harbors deceit.
²⁵ Though his speech is charming, do not believe him,
for seven abominations fill his heart.
²⁶ His malice may be concealed by deception,
but his wickedness will be exposed in the assembly.

²⁷ If a man digs a pit, he will fall into it;
if a man rolls a stone, it will roll back on him.

²⁸ A lying tongue hates those it hurts,
and a flattering mouth works ruin.

Proverbs 27
¹ Do not boast about tomorrow,
for you do not know what a day may bring forth.

² Let another praise you, and not your own mouth;
someone else, and not your own lips.

³ Stone is heavy and sand a burden,
but provocation by a fool is heavier than both.

⁴ Anger is cruel and fury overwhelming,
but who can stand before jealousy?

⁵ Better is open rebuke
than hidden love.

⁶ Wounds from a friend can be trusted,
but an enemy multiplies kisses.

⁷ He who is full loathes honey,
but to the hungry even what is bitter tastes sweet.

⁸ Like a bird that strays from its nest
is a man who strays from his home.

⁹ Perfume and incense bring joy to the heart,
and the pleasantness of one's friend springs from his earnest counsel.

¹⁰ Do not forsake your friend and the friend of your father,
and do not go to your brother's house when disaster strikes you-
better a neighbor nearby than a brother far away.

¹¹ Be wise, my son, and bring joy to my heart;
then I can answer anyone who treats me with contempt.

¹² The prudent see danger and take refuge,
but the simple keep going and suffer for it.

¹³ Take the garment of one who puts up security for a stranger;
hold it in pledge if he does it for a wayward woman.

¹⁴ If a man loudly blesses his neighbor early in the morning,
it will be taken as a curse.

¹⁵ A quarrelsome wife is like
a constant dripping on a rainy day;
¹⁶ restraining her is like restraining the wind
or grasping oil with the hand.

¹⁷ As iron sharpens iron,
so one man sharpens another.

¹⁸ He who tends a fig tree will eat its fruit,
and he who looks after his master will be honored.

¹⁹ As water reflects a face,
so a man's heart reflects the man.

²⁰ Death and Destruction are never satisfied,
and neither are the eyes of man.

²¹ The crucible for silver and the furnace for gold,
but man is tested by the praise he receives.

²² Though you grind a fool in a mortar,
grinding him like grain with a pestle,
you will not remove his folly from him.

²³ Be sure you know the condition of your flocks,
give careful attention to your herds;
²⁴ for riches do not endure forever,
and a crown is not secure for all generations.
²⁵ When the hay is removed and new growth appears
and the grass from the hills is gathered in,
²⁶ the lambs will provide you with clothing,
and the goats with the price of a field.
²⁷ You will have plenty of goats' milk
to feed you and your family
and to nourish your servant girls.

Proverbs 28

¹ The wicked man flees though no one pursues,
but the righteous are as bold as a lion.

² When a country is rebellious, it has many rulers,
but a man of understanding and knowledge maintains order.

³ A ruler who oppresses the poor
is like a driving rain that leaves no crops.

⁴ Those who forsake the law praise the wicked,
but those who keep the law resist them.

⁵ Evil men do not understand justice,
but those who seek the LORD understand it fully.

⁶ Better a poor man whose walk is blameless
than a rich man whose ways are perverse.

⁷ He who keeps the law is a discerning son,
but a companion of gluttons disgraces his father.

⁸ He who increases his wealth by exorbitant interest
amasses it for another, who will be kind to the poor.

⁹ If anyone turns a deaf ear to the law,
even his prayers are detestable.

¹⁰ He who leads the upright along an evil path
will fall into his own trap,
but the blameless will receive a good inheritance.

¹¹ A rich man may be wise in his own eyes,
but a poor man who has discernment sees through him.

¹² When the righteous triumph, there is great elation;
but when the wicked rise to power, men go into hiding.

¹³ He who conceals his sins does not prosper,
but whoever confesses and renounces them finds mercy.

¹⁴ Blessed is the man who always fears the LORD,
but he who hardens his heart falls into trouble.

¹⁵ Like a roaring lion or a charging bear
is a wicked man ruling over a helpless people.

¹⁶ A tyrannical ruler lacks judgment,
but he who hates ill-gotten gain will enjoy a long life.

¹⁷ A man tormented by the guilt of murder
will be a fugitive till death;
let no one support him.

¹⁸ He whose walk is blameless is kept safe,
but he whose ways are perverse will suddenly fall.

¹⁹ He who works his land will have abundant food,
but the one who chases fantasies will have his fill of poverty.

²⁰ A faithful man will be richly blessed,
but one eager to get rich will not go unpunished.

²¹ To show partiality is not good-
yet a man will do wrong for a piece of bread.

²² A stingy man is eager to get rich
and is unaware that poverty awaits him.

²³ He who rebukes a man will in the end gain more favor
than he who has a flattering tongue.

²⁴ He who robs his father or mother
and says, "It's not wrong"-
he is partner to him who destroys.

²⁵ A greedy man stirs up dissension,
but he who trusts in the LORD will prosper.

²⁶ He who trusts in himself is a fool,
but he who walks in wisdom is kept safe.

²⁷ He who gives to the poor will lack nothing,
but he who closes his eyes to them receives many curses.

²⁸ When the wicked rise to power, people go into hiding;
but when the wicked perish, the righteous thrive.

Proverbs 29

[1] A man who remains stiff-necked after many rebukes
will suddenly be destroyed-without remedy.

[2] When the righteous thrive, the people rejoice;
when the wicked rule, the people groan.

[3] A man who loves wisdom brings joy to his father,
but a companion of prostitutes squanders his wealth.

[4] By justice a king gives a country stability,
but one who is greedy for bribes tears it down.

[5] Whoever flatters his neighbor
is spreading a net for his feet.

[6] An evil man is snared by his own sin,
but a righteous one can sing and be glad.

[7] The righteous care about justice for the poor,
but the wicked have no such concern.

[8] Mockers stir up a city,
but wise men turn away anger.

[9] If a wise man goes to court with a fool,
the fool rages and scoffs, and there is no peace.

[10] Bloodthirsty men hate a man of integrity
and seek to kill the upright.

[11] A fool gives full vent to his anger,
but a wise man keeps himself under control.

[12] If a ruler listens to lies,
all his officials become wicked.

[13] The poor man and the oppressor have this in common:
The LORD gives sight to the eyes of both.

¹⁴ If a king judges the poor with fairness,
his throne will always be secure.

¹⁵ The rod of correction imparts wisdom,
but a child left to himself disgraces his mother.

¹⁶ When the wicked thrive, so does sin,
but the righteous will see their downfall.

¹⁷ Discipline your son, and he will give you peace;
he will bring delight to your soul.

¹⁸ Where there is no revelation, the people cast off restraint;
but blessed is he who keeps the law.

¹⁹ A servant cannot be corrected by mere words;
though he understands, he will not respond.

²⁰ Do you see a man who speaks in haste?
There is more hope for a fool than for him.

²¹ If a man pampers his servant from youth,
he will bring grief in the end.

²² An angry man stirs up dissension,
and a hot-tempered one commits many sins.

²³ A man's pride brings him low,
but a man of lowly spirit gains honor.

²⁴ The accomplice of a thief is his own enemy;
he is put under oath and dare not testify.

²⁵ Fear of man will prove to be a snare,
but whoever trusts in the LORD is kept safe.

²⁶ Many seek an audience with a ruler,
but it is from the LORD that man gets justice.

²⁷ The righteous detest the dishonest;
the wicked detest the upright.

Proverbs 30

¹ The sayings of Agur son of Jakeh—an oracle:

This man declared to Ithiel,
to Ithiel and to Ucal:

² "I am the most ignorant of men;
I do not have a man's understanding.
³ I have not learned wisdom,
nor have I knowledge of the Holy One.
⁴ Who has gone up to heaven and come down?
Who has gathered up the wind in the hollow of his hands?
Who has wrapped up the waters in his cloak?
Who has established all the ends of the earth?
What is his name, and the name of his son?
Tell me if you know!

⁵ "Every word of God is flawless;
he is a shield to those who take refuge in him.
⁶ Do not add to his words,
or he will rebuke you and prove you a liar.

⁷ "Two things I ask of you, O LORD;
do not refuse me before I die:
⁸ Keep falsehood and lies far from me;
give me neither poverty nor riches,
but give me only my daily bread.
⁹ Otherwise, I may have too much and disown you
and say, 'Who is the LORD?'
Or I may become poor and steal,
and so dishonor the name of my God.

¹⁰ "Do not slander a servant to his master,
or he will curse you, and you will pay for it.

[11] "There are those who curse their fathers
and do not bless their mothers;
[12] those who are pure in their own eyes
and yet are not cleansed of their filth;
[13] those whose eyes are ever so haughty,
whose glances are so disdainful;
[14] those whose teeth are swords
and whose jaws are set with knives
to devour the poor from the earth,
the needy from among mankind.

[15] "The leech has two daughters.
'Give! Give!' they cry.

"There are three things that are never satisfied,
four that never say, 'Enough!':
[16] the grave, the barren womb,
land, which is never satisfied with water,
and fire, which never says, 'Enough!'

[17] "The eye that mocks a father,
that scorns obedience to a mother,
will be pecked out by the ravens of the valley,
will be eaten by the vultures.

[18] "There are three things that are too amazing for me,
four that I do not understand:
[19] the way of an eagle in the sky,
the way of a snake on a rock,
the way of a ship on the high seas,
and the way of a man with a maiden.

[20] "This is the way of an adulteress:
She eats and wipes her mouth
and says, 'I've done nothing wrong.'

[21] "Under three things the earth trembles,
under four it cannot bear up:

[22] a servant who becomes king,
a fool who is full of food,
[23] an unloved woman who is married,
and a maidservant who displaces her mistress.

[24] "Four things on earth are small,
yet they are extremely wise:
[25] Ants are creatures of little strength,
yet they store up their food in the summer;
[26] coneys are creatures of little power,
yet they make their home in the crags;
[27] locusts have no king,
yet they advance together in ranks;
[28] a lizard can be caught with the hand,
yet it is found in kings' palaces.

[29] "There are three things that are stately in their stride,
four that move with stately bearing:
[30] a lion, mighty among beasts,
who retreats before nothing;
[31] a strutting rooster, a he-goat,
and a king with his army around him.

[32] "If you have played the fool and exalted yourself,
or if you have planned evil,
clap your hand over your mouth!
[33] For as churning the milk produces butter,
and as twisting the nose produces blood,
so stirring up anger produces strife."

Proverbs 31

¹ The sayings of King Lemuel-an oracle his mother taught him:

² "O my son, O son of my womb,
O son of my vows,
³ do not spend your strength on women,
your vigor on those who ruin kings.

⁴ "It is not for kings, O Lemuel-
not for kings to drink wine,
not for rulers to crave beer,
⁵ lest they drink and forget what the law decrees,
and deprive all the oppressed of their rights.
⁶ Give beer to those who are perishing,
wine to those who are in anguish;
⁷ let them drink and forget their poverty
and remember their misery no more.

⁸ "Speak up for those who cannot speak for themselves,
for the rights of all who are destitute.
⁹ Speak up and judge fairly;
defend the rights of the poor and needy."
Epilogue: The Wife of Noble Character
¹⁰ A wife of noble character who can find?
She is worth far more than rubies.
¹¹ Her husband has full confidence in her
and lacks nothing of value.
¹² She brings him good, not harm,
all the days of her life.
¹³ She selects wool and flax
and works with eager hands.
¹⁴ She is like the merchant ships,
bringing her food from afar.
¹⁵ She gets up while it is still dark;
she provides food for her family
and portions for her servant girls.
¹⁶ She considers a field and buys it;
out of her earnings she plants a vineyard.

¹⁷ She sets about her work vigorously;
her arms are strong for her tasks.
¹⁸ She sees that her trading is profitable,
and her lamp does not go out at night.
¹⁹ In her hand she holds the distaff
and grasps the spindle with her fingers.
²⁰ She opens her arms to the poor
and extends her hands to the needy.
²¹ When it snows, she has no fear for her household;
for all of them are clothed in scarlet.
²² She makes coverings for her bed;
she is clothed in fine linen and purple.
²³ Her husband is respected at the city gate,
where he takes his seat among the elders of the land.
²⁴ She makes linen garments and sells them,
and supplies the merchants with sashes.
²⁵ She is clothed with strength and dignity;
she can laugh at the days to come.
²⁶ She speaks with wisdom,
and faithful instruction is on her tongue.
²⁷ She watches over the affairs of her household
and does not eat the bread of idleness.
²⁸ Her children arise and call her blessed;
her husband also, and he praises her:
²⁹ "Many women do noble things,
but you surpass them all."
³⁰ Charm is deceptive, and beauty is fleeting;
but a woman who fears the LORD is to be praised.
³¹ Give her the reward she has earned,
and let her works bring her praise at the city gate. NIV

1 Corinthians 1:18-31

[18] For the word of the cross is foolishness to those who are perishing, but to us who are being saved it is the power of God.

[19] For it is written,

> "I WILL DESTROY THE WISDOM OF THE WISE,
> AND THE CLEVERNESS OF THE CLEVER I WILL SET
> ASIDE."

[20] Where is the wise man? Where is the scribe? Where is the debater of this age? Has not God made foolish the wisdom of the world?

[21] For since in the wisdom of God the world through its wisdom did not come to know God, God was well-pleased through the foolishness of the message preached to save those who believe.

[22] For indeed Jews ask for signs and Greeks search for wisdom;

[23] but we preach Christ crucified, to Jews a stumbling block and to Gentiles foolishness,

[24] but to those who are the called, both Jews and Greeks, Christ the power of God and the wisdom of God.

[25] Because the foolishness of God is wiser than men, and the weakness of God is stronger than men.

[26] For consider your calling, brethren, that there were not many wise according to the flesh, not many mighty, not many noble;

[27] but God has chosen the foolish things of the world to shame the wise, and God has chosen the weak things of the world to shame the things which are strong,

[28] and the base things of the world and the despised God has chosen, the things that are not, so that He may nullify the things that are,

[29] so that no man may boast before God.

[30] But by His doing you are in Christ Jesus, who became to us wisdom from God, and righteousness and sanctification, and redemption,

[31] so that, just as it is written, "LET HIM WHO BOASTS, BOAST IN THE LORD." NASB

1 Corinthians 3:1-23

¹Dear brothers and sisters, when I was with you I couldn't talk to you as I would to mature Christians. I had to talk as though you belonged to this world or as though you were infants in the Christian life. ²I had to feed you with milk and not with solid food, because you couldn't handle anything stronger. And you still aren't ready, ³for you are still controlled by your own sinful desires. You are jealous of one another and quarrel with each other. Doesn't that prove you are controlled by your own desires? You are acting like people who don't belong to the Lord. ⁴When one of you says, "I am a follower of Paul," and another says, "I prefer Apollos," aren't you acting like those who are not Christians?

⁵Who is Apollos, and who is Paul, that we should be the cause of such quarrels? Why, we're only servants. Through us God caused you to believe. Each of us did the work the Lord gave us. ⁶My job was to plant the seed in your hearts, and Apollos watered it, but it was God, not we, who made it grow. ⁷The ones who do the planting or watering aren't important, but God is important because he is the one who makes the seed grow. ⁸The one who plants and the one who waters work as a team with the same purpose. Yet they will be rewarded individually, according to their own hard work. ⁹We work together as partners who belong to God. You are God's field, God's building—not ours.

¹⁰Because of God's special favor to me, I have laid the foundation like an expert builder. Now others are building on it. But whoever is building on this foundation must be very careful. ¹¹For no one can lay any other foundation than the one we already have—Jesus Christ. ¹²Now anyone who builds on that foundation may use gold, silver, jewels, wood, hay, or straw. ¹³But there is going to come a time of testing at the judgment day to see what kind of work each builder has done. Everyone's work will be put through the fire to see whether or not it keeps its value. ¹⁴If the work survives the fire, that builder will receive a reward. ¹⁵But if the work is burned up, the builder will suffer great loss. The builders themselves will be saved, but like someone escaping through a wall of flames.

¹⁶Don't you realize that all of you together are the temple of God and that the Spirit of God lives in you? ¹⁷God will bring ruin upon anyone who ruins this temple. For God's temple is holy, and you Christians are that temple.

¹⁸Stop fooling yourselves. If you think you are wise by this world's standards, you will have to become a fool so you can become wise by God's standards. ¹⁹For the wisdom of this world is foolishness to God. As the Scriptures say,

"God catches those who think they are wise
in their own cleverness."

²⁰And again,

"The Lord knows the thoughts of the wise,
that they are worthless."

²¹So don't take pride in following a particular leader. Everything belongs to you: ²²Paul and Apollos and Peter; the whole world and life and death; the present and the future. Everything belongs to you, ²³and you belong to Christ, and Christ belongs to God. NLT

James 1:2-5

²Consider it a sheer gift, friends, when tests and challenges come at you from all sides. ³You know that under pressure, your faith-life is forced into the open and shows its true colors. ⁴So don't try to get out of anything prematurely. Let it do its work so you become mature and well-developed, not deficient in any way.

⁵If you don't know what you're doing, pray to the Father. He loves to help. You'll get his help, and won't be condescended to when you ask for it. MSG

Luke 2:39-52

³⁹After Joseph and Mary had done everything that the Law of the Lord commands, they returned home to Nazareth in Galilee. ⁴⁰The child Jesus grew. He became strong and wise, and God blessed him.

⁴¹Every year Jesus' parents went to Jerusalem for Passover. ⁴²And when Jesus was twelve years old, they all went there as usual for the celebration. ⁴³After Passover his parents left, but they did not know that Jesus had stayed on in the city. ⁴⁴They thought he was traveling with some other people, and they went a whole daybefore they started looking for him. ⁴⁵When they could not find him with their relatives and friends, they went back to Jerusalem and started looking for him there. ⁴⁶Three days later they found Jesus sitting in the temple, listening to the teachers and asking them questions.

⁴⁷Everyone who heard him was surprised at how much he knew and at the answers he gave. ⁴⁸When his parents found him, they were amazed. His

mother said, "Son, why have you done this to us? Your father and I have been very worried, and we have been searching for you!"
⁴⁹Jesus answered, "Why did you have to look for me? Didn't you know that I would be in my Father's house?" ⁵⁰But they did not understand what he meant. ⁵¹Jesus went back to Nazareth with his parents and obeyed them. His mother kept on thinking about all that had happened. ⁵²Jesus became wise, and he grew strong. God was pleased with him and so were the people. CEV

Ephesians 5:15-21

¹⁵Be very careful, then, how you live—not as unwise but as wise, ¹⁶making the most of every opportunity, because the days are evil. ¹⁷Therefore do not be foolish, but understand what the Lord's will is. ¹⁸Do not get drunk on wine, which leads to debauchery. Instead, be filled with the Spirit. ¹⁹Speak to one another with psalms, hymns and spiritual songs. Sing and make music in your heart to the Lord, ²⁰always giving thanks to God the Father for everything, in the name of our Lord Jesus Christ.
²¹Submit to one another out of reverence for Christ. NIV

2 Timothy 3:14-17

¹⁴But as for you, continue to hold to the things that you have learned and of which you are convinced, knowing from whom you learned [them],
¹⁵And how from your childhood you have had a knowledge of and been acquainted with the sacred Writings, which are able to instruct you and give you the understanding for salvation which comes through faith in Christ Jesus [through the leaning of the entire human personality on God in Christ Jesus in absolute trust and confidence in His power, wisdom, and goodness].
¹⁶Every Scripture is God-breathed (given by His inspiration) and profitable for instruction, for reproof and conviction of sin, for correction of error and discipline in obedience, [and] for training in righteousness (in holy living, in conformity to God's will in thought, purpose, and action),
¹⁷So that the man of God may be complete and proficient, well fitted and thoroughly equipped for every good work. AMP

Psalm 51

6 Behold, You desire truth in the innermost being,
    And in the hidden part You will make me know wisdom. NASB

Psalm 104

24 O LORD, how many are Your works!
    In wisdom You have made them all;
    The earth is full of Your possessions. NASB

Psalm 111

10 The fear of the LORD is the beginning of wisdom;
    A good understanding have all those who do His
        commandments;
    His praise endures forever. NASB

Psalm 119

98 Your commandments make me wiser than my enemies,
    For they are ever mine. NASB

1 Corinthians 1

30 But by His doing you are in Christ Jesus, who became to us wisdom
from God, and righteousness and sanctification, and redemption. NASB

Wise Guys

The Journal

Day 1   Proverbs 1   Date: _____

These are the wise sayings of Solomon, David's son, Israel's king—
Written down so we'll know how to live well and right, to understand what life means and where it's going. (1:1, 2 MSG)

What stands out? A thought, a word, a phrase. _____
_____
_____
_____
_____
_____
_____

What can be worked on today? _____
_____
_____
_____
_____
_____

What are you thinking, dreaming, praying? _____
_____
_____
_____
_____
_____
_____
_____
_____

Day 2   Proverbs 2   Date: _____

These are the proverbs of King Solomon of Israel, the son of David.
You will learn what is right and honest and fair. (1:1,3 CEV)

What stands out? A thought, a word, a phrase. _____

_____

_____

_____

_____

_____

_____

What can be worked on today? _____

_____

_____

_____

_____

_____

_____

What are you thinking, dreaming, praying? _____

_____

_____

_____

_____

_____

_____

_____

_____

_____

_____

Day 3   Proverbs 3   Date: _____

If you are already wise, you will become even wiser.
And if you are smart, you will learn to understand. (1:5 CEV)

What stands out? A thought, a word, a phrase. _____

_____

_____

_____

_____

_____

_____

What can be worked on today? _____

_____

_____

_____

_____

_____

_____

What are you thinking, dreaming, praying? _____

_____

_____

_____

_____

_____

_____

_____

_____

_____

Day 4   Proverbs 4   Date: _____

For the LORD gives wisdom,
and from his mouth come knowledge and understanding. (2:6 NIV)

What stands out? A thought, a word, a phrase. _____

_____

_____

_____

_____

_____

_____

What can be worked on today? _____

_____

_____

_____

_____

_____

What are you thinking, dreaming, praying? _____

_____

_____

_____

_____

_____

_____

_____

_____

_____

Day 5   Proverbs 5   Date: _____

For skillful and godly Wisdom shall enter into your heart, and
knowledge shall be pleasant to you. (2:10 AMP)

What stands out? A thought, a word, a phrase. _____

_____

_____

_____

_____

_____

_____

What can be worked on today? _____

_____

_____

_____

_____

_____

_____

What are you thinking, dreaming, praying? _____

_____

_____

_____

_____

_____

_____

_____

_____

_____

Day 6   Proverbs 6   Date: _____

Thoughtfulness doth watch over thee, Understanding doth keep thee... (2:11 YLT)

What stands out? A thought, a word, a phrase. _____

_____

_____

_____

_____

_____

_____

What can be worked on today? _____

_____

_____

_____

_____

_____

_____

What are you thinking, dreaming, praying? _____

_____

_____

_____

_____

_____

_____

_____

_____

_____

_____

Trust in the LORD with all your heart
    And do not lean on your own understanding... (3:5 NASB)

What stands out? A thought, a word, a phrase. _____

_____

_____

_____

_____

_____

_____

What can be worked on today? _____

_____

_____

_____

_____

_____

_____

What are you thinking, dreaming, praying? _____

_____

_____

_____

_____

_____

_____

_____

_____

_____

Day 8   Proverbs 8   Date: _____

In all your ways acknowledge Him,
And He will make your paths straight. (3:6 NASB)

What stands out? A thought, a word, a phrase. _____

_____

_____

_____

_____

_____

_____

What can be worked on today? _____

_____

_____

_____

_____

_____

_____

What are you thinking, dreaming, praying? _____

_____

_____

_____

_____

_____

_____

_____

_____

_____

_____

Day 9   Proverbs 9   Date: _____

Happy (blessed, fortunate, enviable) is the man who finds skillful and godly Wisdom, and the man who gets understanding [drawing it forth from God's Word and life's experiences].... (3:13 AMP)

What stands out? A thought, a word, a phrase. _____

_____

_____

_____

_____

_____

_____

What can be worked on today? _____

_____

_____

_____

_____

_____

What are you thinking, dreaming, praying? _____

_____

_____

_____

_____

_____

_____

_____

_____

Get wisdom! Get understanding! Do not forget, nor turn away
from the words of my mouth. (4:15 NKJV)

What stands out? A thought, a word, a phrase. _____

_____

_____

_____

_____

_____

_____

What can be worked on today? _____

_____

_____

_____

_____

_____

What are you thinking, dreaming, praying? _____

_____

_____

_____

_____

_____

_____

_____

_____

_____

Day 11   Proverbs 11   Date: _____

Never walk away from Wisdom—she guards your life;
love her—she keeps her eye on you. (4:6 MSG)

What stands out? A thought, a word, a phrase. _____

_____

_____

_____

_____

_____

_____

What can be worked on today? _____

_____

_____

_____

_____

_____

_____

What are you thinking, dreaming, praying? _____

_____

_____

_____

_____

_____

_____

_____

_____

_____

Day 12   Proverbs 12   Date: _____

Wisdom is supreme; therefore get wisdom.
Though it cost all you have, get understanding. (4:7 NIV)

What stands out? A thought, a word, a phrase. _____

_____

_____

_____

_____

_____

What can be worked on today? _____

_____

_____

_____

_____

_____

What are you thinking, dreaming, praying? _____

_____

_____

_____

_____

_____

_____

_____

_____

_____

Day 13   Proverbs 13   Date: _____

I guide you in the way of wisdom
and lead you along straight paths. (4:11 NIV)

What stands out? A thought, a word, a phrase. _____

_____

_____

_____

_____

_____

_____

What can be worked on today? _____

_____

_____

_____

_____

_____

_____

What are you thinking, dreaming, praying? _____

_____

_____

_____

_____

_____

_____

_____

_____

_____

Day 14   Proverbs 14   Date: _____

When you walk, your steps shall not be hampered [your path will be clear and open]; and when you run, you shall not stumble. (4:12 AMP)

What stands out? A thought, a word, a phrase. _____

_____

_____

_____

_____

_____

_____

What can be worked on today? _____

_____

_____

_____

_____

_____

What are you thinking, dreaming, praying? _____

_____

_____

_____

_____

_____

_____

_____

_____

_____

Those who discover these words live, really live;
body and soul, they're bursting with health. (4:22 MSG)

What stands out? A thought, a word, a phrase. _____

_____

_____

_____

_____

_____

_____

What can be worked on today? _____

_____

_____

_____

_____

_____

_____

What are you thinking, dreaming, praying? _____

_____

_____

_____

_____

_____

_____

_____

_____

_____

_____

Day 16   Proverbs 16 ·   Date: _____

When you go, they [the words of your parents' God] shall lead
you; when you sleep, they shall keep you; and when you waken,
they shall talk with you. (6:22 AMP)

What stands out? A thought, a word, a phrase. _____

_____

_____

_____

_____

_____

_____

What can be worked on today? _____

_____

_____

_____

_____

_____

_____

What are you thinking, dreaming, praying? _____

_____

_____

_____

_____

_____

_____

_____

_____

_____

Day 17   Proverbs 17   Date: _____

The Law of the Lord is a lamp, and its teachings shine brightly.
Correction and self-control will lead you through life. (6:23 CEV)

What stands out? A thought, a word, a phrase. _____

_____

_____

_____

_____

_____

_____

What can be worked on today? _____

_____

_____

_____

_____

_____

_____

What are you thinking, dreaming, praying? _____

_____

_____

_____

_____

_____

_____

_____

_____

_____

Day 18   **Proverbs 18**   Date: _____

Go to the ant, O sluggard;
  consider her ways, and be wise. (6:6 ESV)

What stands out? A thought, a word, a phrase. _____

_____

_____

_____

_____

_____

_____

What can be worked on today? _____

_____

_____

_____

_____

_____

What are you thinking, dreaming, praying? _____

_____

_____

_____

_____

_____

_____

_____

_____

_____

Day 19   Proverbs 19   Date: _____

My son, pay close attention and don't forget what I tell you to do.
(7:1 CEV)

What stands out? A thought, a word, a phrase. _____
_____
_____
_____
_____
_____
_____
_____

What can be worked on today? _____
_____
_____
_____
_____
_____
_____

What are you thinking, dreaming, praying? _____
_____
_____
_____
_____
_____
_____
_____
_____
_____
_____

Bind them on your fingers;
    Write them on the tablet of your heart. (7:3 NKJV)

What stands out? A thought, a word, a phrase. _____

_____

_____

_____

_____

_____

_____

What can be worked on today? _____

_____

_____

_____

_____

_____

_____

What are you thinking, dreaming, praying? _____

_____

_____

_____

_____

_____

_____

_____

_____

_____

Day 21   Proverbs 21   Date: _____

Love wisdom like a sister; make insight a beloved member of your
family. (7:4 NLT)

What stands out? A thought, a word, a phrase. _____
_____
_____
_____
_____
_____
_____

What can be worked on today? _____
_____
_____
_____
_____
_____
_____

What are you thinking, dreaming, praying? _____
_____
_____
_____
_____
_____
_____
_____
_____
_____

I love those who love me;
And those who diligently seek me will find me. (8:17 NASB)

What stands out? A thought, a word, a phrase. _____

_____

_____

_____

_____

_____

_____

What can be worked on today? _____

_____

_____

_____

_____

_____

_____

What are you thinking, dreaming, praying? _____

_____

_____

_____

_____

_____

_____

_____

_____

_____

_____

Day 23   Proverbs 23   Date: _____

Blessed the man, blessed the woman, who listens to me,
awake and ready for me each morning,
alert and responsive as I start my day's work. (8:34 MSG)

What stands out? A thought, a word, a phrase. _____

_____

_____

_____

_____

_____

_____

What can be worked on today? _____

_____

_____

_____

_____

_____

_____

What are you thinking, dreaming, praying? _____

_____

_____

_____

_____

_____

_____

_____

_____

For whoever finds me finds life,
    And obtains favor from the LORD. (8:35 NKJV)

What stands out? A thought, a word, a phrase. _____

_____

_____

_____

_____

_____

_____

What can be worked on today? _____

_____

_____

_____

_____

_____

What are you thinking, dreaming, praying? _____

_____

_____

_____

_____

_____

_____

_____

_____

_____

Instruct a wise man and he will be wiser still;
teach a righteous man and he will add to his learning. (9:9 NIV)

What stands out? A thought, a word, a phrase. _____

_____

_____

_____

_____

_____

_____

What can be worked on today? _____

_____

_____

_____

_____

_____

What are you thinking, dreaming, praying? _____

_____

_____

_____

_____

_____

_____

_____

_____

Day 26　　　　**Proverbs 26**　　　　Date: _____

The fear of the LORD is the beginning of wisdom,
and knowledge of the Holy One is understanding. (9:10 NIV)

What stands out? A thought, a word, a phrase. _____

_____

_____

_____

_____

_____

_____

What can be worked on today? _____

_____

_____

_____

_____

_____

What are you thinking, dreaming, praying? _____

_____

_____

_____

_____

_____

_____

_____

_____

_____

_____

Day 27   Proverbs 27   Date: _____

For through me your days will be many,
and years will be added to your life. (9:11 NIV)

What stands out? A thought, a word, a phrase. _____

_____
_____
_____
_____
_____
_____

What can be worked on today? _____

_____
_____
_____
_____
_____
_____

What are you thinking, dreaming, praying? _____

_____
_____
_____
_____
_____
_____
_____
_____
_____
_____

Lazy people are soon poor; hard workers get rich. (10:4 NLT)

What stands out? A thought, a word, a phrase. _____
_____
_____
_____
_____
_____
_____

What can be worked on today? _____
_____
_____
_____
_____
_____
_____

What are you thinking, dreaming, praying? _____
_____
_____
_____
_____
_____
_____
_____
_____
_____
_____

Day 29   Proverbs 29   Date: _____

At harvest season it's smart to work hard, but stupid to sleep.
(10:5 CEV)

What stands out? A thought, a word, a phrase. _____

_____

_____

_____

_____

_____

What can be worked on today? _____

_____

_____

_____

_____

_____

What are you thinking, dreaming, praying? _____

_____

_____

_____

_____

_____

_____

_____

_____

Day 30   Proverbs 30   Date: _____

When words are many, sin is not absent,
but he who holds his tongue is wise. (10:19 NIV)

What stands out? A thought, a word, a phrase. _____
_____
_____
_____
_____
_____
_____

What can be worked on today? _____
_____
_____
_____
_____
_____

What are you thinking, dreaming, praying? _____
_____
_____
_____
_____
_____
_____
_____
_____
_____

He who belittles and despises his neighbor lacks sense, but a man of understanding keeps silent. (11:12 AMP)

What stands out? A thought, a word, a phrase. _____

_____

_____

_____

_____

_____

_____

What can be worked on today? _____

_____

_____

_____

_____

_____

_____

What are you thinking, dreaming, praying? _____

_____

_____

_____

_____

_____

_____

_____

_____

_____

_____

A gossip goes around revealing secrets, but those who are trustworthy can keep a confidence. (11:13 NLT)

What stands out? A thought, a word, a phrase. _____

_____

_____

_____

_____

_____

_____

What can be worked on today? _____

_____

_____

_____

_____

_____

_____

What are you thinking, dreaming, praying? _____

_____

_____

_____

_____

_____

_____

_____

_____

_____

_____

Day 33   I Corinthians 3:1-23   Date: _____

Where there is no guidance, a people falls,
   but in an abundance of counselors there is safety. (11:14 ESV)

What stands out? A thought, a word, a phrase. _____

_____

_____

_____

_____

_____

_____

What can be worked on today? _____

_____

_____

_____

_____

_____

_____

What are you thinking, dreaming, praying? _____

_____

_____

_____

_____

_____

_____

_____

_____

_____

WHOEVER LOVES instruction and correction loves knowledge, but he who hates reproof is like a brute beast, stupid and indiscriminating. (12:1 AMP)

What stands out? A thought, a word, a phrase. _____

_____

_____

_____

_____

_____

_____

What can be worked on today? _____

_____

_____

_____

_____

_____

What are you thinking, dreaming, praying? _____

_____

_____

_____

_____

_____

_____

_____

_____

_____

A person who talks sense is honored;
airheads are held in contempt. (12:8 MSG)

What stands out? A thought, a word, a phrase. _____

_____

_____

_____

_____

_____

_____

What can be worked on today? _____

_____

_____

_____

_____

_____

_____

What are you thinking, dreaming, praying? _____

_____

_____

_____

_____

_____

_____

_____

_____

_____

_____

Day 36   Proverbs 3   Date: _____

A righteous man cares for the needs of his animal,
but the kindest acts of the wicked are cruel. (12:10 NIV)

What stands out? A thought, a word, a phrase. _____

_____
_____
_____
_____
_____
_____

What can be worked on today? _____

_____
_____
_____
_____
_____
_____

What are you thinking, dreaming, praying? _____

_____
_____
_____
_____
_____
_____
_____
_____
_____
_____

Those who control their tongue will have a long life; a quick retort
can ruin everything. (13:3 NLT)

What stands out? A thought, a word, a phrase. _____
_____
_____
_____
_____
_____
_____

What can be worked on today? _____
_____
_____
_____
_____
_____
_____

What are you thinking, dreaming, praying? _____
_____
_____
_____
_____
_____
_____
_____
_____
_____

Arrogant know-it-alls stir up discord, but wise men and women listen to each other's counsel. (13:10 MSG)

What stands out? A thought, a word, a phrase. _____

_____

_____

_____

_____

_____

_____

What can be worked on today? _____

_____

_____

_____

_____

_____

What are you thinking, dreaming, praying? _____

_____

_____

_____

_____

_____

_____

_____

_____

_____

Day 39   Proverbs 6   Date: _____

He who walks [as a companion] with wise men is wise, but he who associates with [self-confident] fools is [a fool himself and] shall smart for it. (13:20 AMP)

What stands out? A thought, a word, a phrase. _____

_____

_____

_____

_____

_____

_____

What can be worked on today? _____

_____

_____

_____

_____

_____

_____

What are you thinking, dreaming, praying? _____

_____

_____

_____

_____

_____

_____

_____

_____

_____

The naive believes everything,
> But the sensible man considers his steps. (14:15 NASB)

What stands out? A thought, a word, a phrase. _____

_____

_____

_____

_____

_____

_____

What can be worked on today? _____

_____

_____

_____

_____

_____

_____

What are you thinking, dreaming, praying? _____

_____

_____

_____

_____

_____

_____

_____

_____

_____

_____

He who despises his neighbor sins,
    But happy is he who is gracious to the poor. (14:21 NASB)

What stands out? A thought, a word, a phrase. _____

_____

_____

_____

_____

_____

_____

What can be worked on today? _____

_____

_____

_____

_____

_____

What are you thinking, dreaming, praying? _____

_____

_____

_____

_____

_____

_____

_____

_____

_____

Whoever oppresses a poor man insults his Maker,
but he who is generous to the needy honors him. (14:31 ESV)

What stands out? A thought, a word, a phrase. _____

_____

_____

_____

_____

_____

_____

What can be worked on today? _____

_____

_____

_____

_____

_____

What are you thinking, dreaming, praying? _____

_____

_____

_____

_____

_____

_____

_____

_____

_____

_____

Day 43   Proverbs 10   Date: _____

A soft answer turns away wrath,
    but a harsh word stirs up anger. (15:1 ESV)

What stands out? A thought, a word, a phrase. _____
_____
_____
_____
_____
_____
_____

What can be worked on today? _____
_____
_____
_____
_____
_____

What are you thinking, dreaming, praying? _____
_____
_____
_____
_____
_____
_____
_____
_____
_____

Day 44   Proverbs 11   Date: _____

Kind words heal and help;
cutting words wound and maim. (15:4 MSG)

What stands out? A thought, a word, a phrase. _____

_____

_____

_____

_____

_____

_____

What can be worked on today? _____

_____

_____

_____

_____

_____

What are you thinking, dreaming, praying? _____

_____

_____

_____

_____

_____

_____

_____

_____

_____

Without counsel, plans go awry,
    But in the multitude of counselors they are established.
    (15:22 NKJV)

What stands out? A thought, a word, a phrase. _____

_____

_____

_____

_____

_____

_____

What can be worked on today? _____

_____

_____

_____

_____

_____

_____

What are you thinking, dreaming, praying? _____

_____

_____

_____

_____

_____

_____

_____

_____

_____

Roll your works upon the Lord [commit and trust them wholly to Him; He will cause your thoughts to become agreeable to His will, and] so shall your plans be established and succeed. (16:3 AMP)

What stands out? A thought, a word, a phrase. _____

_____

_____

_____

_____

_____

_____

What can be worked on today? _____

_____

_____

_____

_____

_____

_____

What are you thinking, dreaming, praying? _____

_____

_____

_____

_____

_____

_____

_____

_____

_____

The mind of man plans his way,
But the LORD directs his steps. (16:9 NASB)

What stands out? A thought, a word, a phrase. _____

_____

_____

_____

_____

_____

_____

What can be worked on today? _____

_____

_____

_____

_____

_____

_____

What are you thinking, dreaming, praying? _____

_____

_____

_____

_____

_____

_____

_____

_____

_____

Day 48   Proverbs 15   Date: _____

Kind words are like honey—they cheer you up and make you feel strong. (16:24 CEV)

What stands out? A thought, a word, a phrase. _____

_____

_____

_____

_____

_____

_____

What can be worked on today? _____

_____

_____

_____

_____

_____

What are you thinking, dreaming, praying? _____

_____

_____

_____

_____

_____

_____

_____

_____

_____

Day 49   Proverbs 16   Date: _____

Beginning a quarrel is like opening a floodgate, so drop the matter before a dispute breaks out. (17:14 NLT)

What stands out? A thought, a word, a phrase. _____

_____

_____

_____

_____

_____

_____

What can be worked on today? _____

_____

_____

_____

_____

_____

_____

What are you thinking, dreaming, praying? _____

_____

_____

_____

_____

_____

_____

_____

_____

_____

Day 50   Proverbs 17   Date: _____

A cheerful heart is good medicine,
but a crushed spirit dries up the bones. (17:22 NIV)

What stands out? A thought, a word, a phrase. _____

_____

_____

_____

_____

_____

_____

What can be worked on today? _____

_____

_____

_____

_____

_____

What are you thinking, dreaming, praying? _____

_____

_____

_____

_____

_____

_____

_____

_____

_____

_____

Day 51   Proverbs 18   Date: _____

Even fools are thought to be wise when they keep silent; when they keep their mouths shut, they seem intelligent. (17:28 NLT)

What stands out? A thought, a word, a phrase. _____

_____

_____

_____

_____

_____

_____

What can be worked on today? _____

_____

_____

_____

_____

_____

_____

What are you thinking, dreaming, praying? _____

_____

_____

_____

_____

_____

_____

_____

_____

_____

Day 52   Proverbs 19   Date: _____

A gift opens the way for the giver
and ushers him into the presence of the great. (18:16 NIV)

What stands out? A thought, a word, a phrase. _____

_____

_____

_____

_____

_____

_____

What can be worked on today? _____

_____

_____

_____

_____

_____

What are you thinking, dreaming, praying? _____

_____

_____

_____

_____

_____

_____

_____

_____

_____

Day 53   Proverbs 20   Date: _____

Words kill, words give life;
they're either poison or fruit—you choose. (18:21 MSG)

What stands out? A thought, a word, a phrase. _____

_____

_____

_____

_____

_____

_____

What can be worked on today? _____

_____

_____

_____

_____

_____

_____

What are you thinking, dreaming, praying? _____

_____

_____

_____

_____

_____

_____

_____

_____

_____

A man's greatest treasure is his wife—
she is a gift from the LORD. (18:22 ESV)

What stands out? A thought, a word, a phrase. _____

_____

_____

_____

_____

_____

_____

What can be worked on today? _____

_____

_____

_____

_____

_____

What are you thinking, dreaming, praying? _____

_____

_____

_____

_____

_____

_____

_____

_____

_____

Day 55   Proverbs 22   Date: _____

Desire without knowledge is not good,
    and whoever makes haste with his feet misses his way.   (19:2 ESV)

What stands out? A thought, a word, a phrase. _____

_____

_____

_____

_____

_____

_____

What can be worked on today? _____

_____

_____

_____

_____

_____

_____

What are you thinking, dreaming, praying? _____

_____

_____

_____

_____

_____

_____

_____

_____

To acquire wisdom is to love oneself; people who cherish under-standing will prosper. (19:8 NLT)

What stands out? A thought, a word, a phrase. _____

_____

_____

_____

_____

_____

_____

What can be worked on today? _____

_____

_____

_____

_____

_____

_____

What are you thinking, dreaming, praying? _____

_____

_____

_____

_____

_____

_____

_____

_____

_____

He who is kind to the poor lends to the LORD,
and he will reward him for what he has done. (19:17 NIV)

What stands out? A thought, a word, a phrase. _____

_____

_____

_____

_____

_____

_____

What can be worked on today? _____

_____

_____

_____

_____

_____

What are you thinking, dreaming, praying? _____

_____

_____

_____

_____

_____

_____

_____

_____

_____

Wine produces mockers; liquor leads to brawls. Whoever is led astray by drink cannot be wise. (20:1 NLT)

What stands out? A thought, a word, a phrase. _____

_____

_____

_____

_____

_____

_____

What can be worked on today? _____

_____

_____

_____

_____

_____

What are you thinking, dreaming, praying? _____

_____

_____

_____

_____

_____

_____

_____

_____

_____

_____

Day 59   Proverbs 26   Date: _____

It's a mark of good character to avert quarrels,
but fools love to pick fights. (20:3 MSG)

What stands out? A thought, a word, a phrase. _____

_____

_____

_____

_____

_____

_____

What can be worked on today? _____

_____

_____

_____

_____

_____

What are you thinking, dreaming, praying? _____

_____

_____

_____

_____

_____

_____

_____

_____

_____

A gossip betrays a confidence;
so avoid a man who talks too much. (20:19 NIV)

What stands out? A thought, a word, a phrase. _____

_____

_____

_____

_____

_____

_____

What can be worked on today? _____

_____

_____

_____

_____

_____

What are you thinking, dreaming, praying? _____

_____

_____

_____

_____

_____

_____

_____

_____

_____

_____

Day 61   Proverbs 28   Date: _____

The king's heart is like channels of water in the hand of the LORD;
He turns it wherever He wishes. (21:1 NASB)

What stands out? A thought, a word, a phrase. _____
_____
_____
_____
_____
_____
_____

What can be worked on today? _____
_____
_____
_____
_____
_____
_____

What are you thinking, dreaming, praying? _____
_____
_____
_____
_____
_____
_____
_____
_____
_____
_____

Whoever shuts his ears to the cry of the poor
    Will also cry himself and not be heard. (21:13 NKJV)

What stands out? A thought, a word, a phrase. _____

_____

_____

_____

_____

_____

_____

What can be worked on today? _____

_____

_____

_____

_____

_____

_____

What are you thinking, dreaming, praying? _____

_____

_____

_____

_____

_____

_____

_____

_____

_____

_____

Day 63   Proverbs 30   Date: _____

He who guards his mouth and his tongue,
        Guards his soul from troubles. (21:23 NASB)

What stands out? A thought, a word, a phrase. _____
_____
_____
_____
_____
_____
_____

What can be worked on today? _____
_____
_____
_____
_____
_____
_____

What are you thinking, dreaming, praying? _____
_____
_____
_____
_____
_____
_____
_____
_____
_____
_____

A good name is more desirable than great riches;
to be esteemed is better than silver or gold. (22:1 NIV)

What stands out? A thought, a word, a phrase. _____

_____

_____

_____

_____

_____

_____

What can be worked on today? _____

_____

_____

_____

_____

_____

What are you thinking, dreaming, praying? _____

_____

_____

_____

_____

_____

_____

_____

_____

_____

A generous man will himself be blessed,
for he shares his food with the poor. (22:9 NIV)

What stands out? A thought, a word, a phrase. _____

_____

_____

_____

_____

_____

_____

What can be worked on today? _____

_____

_____

_____

_____

_____

_____

What are you thinking, dreaming, praying? _____

_____

_____

_____

_____

_____

_____

_____

_____

_____

_____

Do you see a man skillful in his work?
  He will stand before kings;
  he will not stand before obscure men. (22:29 ESV)

What stands out? A thought, a word, a phrase. _____

_____

_____

_____

_____

_____

_____

What can be worked on today? _____

_____

_____

_____

_____

_____

What are you thinking, dreaming, praying? _____

_____

_____

_____

_____

_____

_____

_____

_____

Do not wear yourself out to get rich;
have the wisdom to show restraint. (23:4 NIV)

What stands out? A thought, a word, a phrase. _____

_____

_____

_____

_____

_____

_____

What can be worked on today? _____

_____

_____

_____

_____

_____

What are you thinking, dreaming, praying? _____

_____

_____

_____

_____

_____

_____

_____

_____

My son, if your heart is wise,
    My heart will rejoice—indeed, I myself;   (23:15 NKJV)

What stands out? A thought, a word, a phrase. _____

_____

_____

_____

_____

_____

What can be worked on today? _____

_____

_____

_____

_____

_____

What are you thinking, dreaming, praying? _____

_____

_____

_____

_____

_____

_____

_____

_____

_____

Day 69   Proverbs 3   Date: _____

Don't drink too much wine and get drunk;
don't eat too much food and get fat. (23:20 MSG)

What stands out? A thought, a word, a phrase. _____

_____
_____
_____
_____
_____
_____

What can be worked on today? _____

_____
_____
_____
_____
_____
_____

What are you thinking, dreaming, praying? _____

_____
_____
_____
_____
_____
_____
_____
_____
_____

A wise man is strong,
    Yes, a man of knowledge increases strength. (24:5 NKJV)

What stands out? A thought, a word, a phrase. _____

_____

_____

_____

_____

_____

_____

What can be worked on today? _____

_____

_____

_____

_____

_____

_____

What are you thinking, dreaming, praying? _____

_____

_____

_____

_____

_____

_____

_____

_____

_____

For by wise guidance you will wage war,
    And in abundance of counselors there is victory. (24:6 NASB)

What stands out? A thought, a word, a phrase. _____

_____

_____

_____

_____

_____

_____

What can be worked on today? _____

_____

_____

_____

_____

_____

_____

What are you thinking, dreaming, praying? _____

_____

_____

_____

_____

_____

_____

_____

_____

_____

_____

Day 72   **Proverbs 6**   Date: _____

Know that wisdom is such to your soul;
   if you find it, there will be a future,
   and your hope will not be cut off. (24:14 ESV)

What stands out? A thought, a word, a phrase. _____

_____

_____

_____

_____

_____

_____

What can be worked on today? _____

_____

_____

_____

_____

_____

_____

What are you thinking, dreaming, praying? _____

_____

_____

_____

_____

_____

_____

_____

_____

_____

Day 73   Proverbs 7   Date: _____

The right word at the right time
is like precious gold set in silver. (25:11 CEV)

What stands out? A thought, a word, a phrase. _____

_____

_____

_____

_____

_____

_____

What can be worked on today? _____

_____

_____

_____

_____

_____

What are you thinking, dreaming, praying? _____

_____

_____

_____

_____

_____

_____

_____

_____

_____

Day 74 Proverbs 8 Date: _____

Through patience a ruler can be persuaded,
and a gentle tongue can break a bone. (25:15 NIV)

What stands out? A thought, a word, a phrase. _____
_____
_____
_____
_____
_____
_____

What can be worked on today? _____
_____
_____
_____
_____
_____

What are you thinking, dreaming, praying? _____
_____
_____
_____
_____
_____
_____
_____
_____
_____

Day 75   Proverbs 9   Date: _____

Let your foot seldom be in your neighbor's house, lest he become
tired of you and hate you. (25:17 AMP)

What stands out? A thought, a word, a phrase. _____

_____

_____

_____

_____

_____

_____

What can be worked on today? _____

_____

_____

_____

_____

_____

_____

What are you thinking, dreaming, praying? _____

_____

_____

_____

_____

_____

_____

_____

_____

_____

Like a madman shooting
firebrands or deadly arrows
is a man who deceives his neighbor
and says, "I was only joking!" (26:18,19 NIV)

What stands out? A thought, a word, a phrase. _____

_____

_____

_____

_____

_____

_____

What can be worked on today? _____

_____

_____

_____

_____

_____

What are you thinking, dreaming, praying? _____

_____

_____

_____

_____

_____

_____

_____

_____

Day 77   Proverbs 11   Date: _____

Fire goes out for lack of fuel, and quarrels disappear when gossip stops. (26:20 NLT)

What stands out? A thought, a word, a phrase. _____
_____
_____
_____
_____
_____
_____

What can be worked on today? _____
_____
_____
_____
_____
_____
_____

What are you thinking, dreaming, praying? _____
_____
_____
_____
_____
_____
_____
_____
_____
_____

Day 78   Proverbs 12   Date: _____

As the door turns on its hinges,
    So does the sluggard on his bed. (26:14 NASB)

What stands out? A thought, a word, a phrase. _____
_____
_____
_____
_____
_____
_____

What can be worked on today? _____
_____
_____
_____
_____
_____
_____

What are you thinking, dreaming, praying? _____
_____
_____
_____
_____
_____
_____
_____
_____
_____
_____

Let another man praise you, and not your own mouth;
   A stranger, and not your own lips. (27:2 NKJV)

What stands out? A thought, a word, a phrase. _____

_____

_____

_____

_____

_____

_____

What can be worked on today? _____

_____

_____

_____

_____

_____

_____

What are you thinking, dreaming, praying? _____

_____

_____

_____

_____

_____

_____

_____

_____

_____

Faithful are the wounds of a friend,
　　But deceitful are the kisses of an enemy.　(27:6 NASB)

What stands out? A thought, a word, a phrase. _____

_____

_____

_____

_____

_____

_____

What can be worked on today? _____

_____

_____

_____

_____

_____

What are you thinking, dreaming, praying? _____

_____

_____

_____

_____

_____

_____

_____

_____

_____

Day 81   Proverbs 15   Date: _____

Iron sharpens iron,
   and one man sharpens another. (27:17 ESV)

What stands out? A thought, a word, a phrase. _____

_____

_____

_____

_____

_____

_____

What can be worked on today? _____

_____

_____

_____

_____

_____

_____

What are you thinking, dreaming, praying? _____

_____

_____

_____

_____

_____

_____

_____

_____

_____

_____

Day 82   **Proverbs 16**   Date: _____

The rich think they know it all,
but the poor can see right through them. (28:11 MSG)

What stands out? A thought, a word, a phrase. _____

_____

_____

_____

_____

_____

_____

What can be worked on today? _____

_____

_____

_____

_____

_____

What are you thinking, dreaming, praying? _____

_____

_____

_____

_____

_____

_____

_____

_____

_____

Day 83   Proverbs 17   Date: _____

Work hard, and you will have a lot of food;
waste time, and you will have a lot of trouble. (28:19 CEV)

What stands out? A thought, a word, a phrase. _____

_____

_____

_____

_____

_____

_____

What can be worked on today? _____

_____

_____

_____

_____

_____

_____

What are you thinking, dreaming, praying? _____

_____

_____

_____

_____

_____

_____

_____

_____

_____

_____

He who gives to the poor will not want, but he who hides his eyes [from their want] will have many a curse. (28:27 AMP)

What stands out? A thought, a word, a phrase. _____

_____

_____

_____

_____

_____

_____

What can be worked on today? _____

_____

_____

_____

_____

_____

What are you thinking, dreaming, praying? _____

_____

_____

_____

_____

_____

_____

_____

_____

_____

Men of scorning ensnare a city,
And the wise turn back anger. (29:8 YLT)

What stands out? A thought, a word, a phrase. _____

_____

_____

_____

_____

_____

_____

What can be worked on today? _____

_____

_____

_____

_____

_____

_____

What are you thinking, dreaming, praying? _____

_____

_____

_____

_____

_____

_____

_____

_____

_____

_____

Day 86   **Proverbs 20**   Date: _____

A fool always loses his temper,
　　But a wise man holds it back. (29:11 NASB)

What stands out? A thought, a word, a phrase. _____
_____
_____
_____
_____
_____
_____

What can be worked on today? _____
_____
_____
_____
_____
_____

What are you thinking, dreaming, praying? _____
_____
_____
_____
_____
_____
_____
_____
_____
_____

Do you see a man hasty in his words?
  There is more hope for a fool than for him.   (29:20 NKJV)

What stands out? A thought, a word, a phrase. _____

_____

_____

_____

_____

_____

_____

What can be worked on today? _____

_____

_____

_____

_____

_____

_____

What are you thinking, dreaming, praying? _____

_____

_____

_____

_____

_____

_____

_____

_____

_____

For the LORD gives wisdom,
and from his mouth come knowledge and understanding. (2:6 NIV)

What stands out? A thought, a word, a phrase. _____

_____

_____

_____

_____

_____

What can be worked on today? _____

_____

_____

_____

_____

_____

What are you thinking, dreaming, praying? _____

_____

_____

_____

_____

_____

_____

_____

_____

_____

Banish lies from my lips
and liars from my presence.
Give me enough food to live on,
neither too much nor too little. (30:8 MSG)

What stands out? A thought, a word, a phrase. _____
_____
_____
_____
_____
_____
_____

What can be worked on today? _____
_____
_____
_____
_____
_____
_____

What are you thinking, dreaming, praying? _____
_____
_____
_____
_____
_____
_____
_____
_____

Above all else, guard your heart, for it affects everything you do.
(4:23 NLT)

What stands out? A thought, a word, a phrase. _____

_____

_____

_____

_____

_____

_____

What can be worked on today? _____

_____

_____

_____

_____

_____

_____

What are you thinking, dreaming, praying? _____

_____

_____

_____

_____

_____

_____

_____

_____

_____

Kings and leaders
should not get drunk
or even want to drink. (31:4 CEV)

What stands out? A thought, a word, a phrase. _____

_____

_____

_____

_____

_____

_____

What can be worked on today? _____

_____

_____

_____

_____

_____

_____

What are you thinking, dreaming, praying? _____

_____

_____

_____

_____

_____

_____

_____

_____

Lest, hung over, they don't know right from wrong,
and the people who depend on them are hurt. (31:4 MSG)

What stands out? A thought, a word, a phrase. _____

_____

_____

_____

_____

_____

_____

What can be worked on today? _____

_____

_____

_____

_____

_____

_____

What are you thinking, dreaming, praying? _____

_____

_____

_____

_____

_____

_____

_____

_____

_____

_____

A capable, intelligent, and virtuous woman—who is he who can find her? She is far more precious than jewels and her value is far above rubies or pearls. (31:10 AMP)

What stands out? A thought, a word, a phrase. _____

_____

_____

_____

_____

_____

_____

What can be worked on today? _____

_____

_____

_____

_____

_____

What are you thinking, dreaming, praying? _____

_____

_____

_____

_____

_____

_____

_____

_____

Day 94   Proverbs 28   Date: _____

If any of you is deficient in wisdom, let him ask of the giving God [Who gives] to everyone liberally and ungrudgingly, without reproaching or faultfinding, and it will be given him. (James 1:5 AMP)

What stands out? A thought, a word, a phrase. _____

_____

_____

_____

_____

_____

_____

What can be worked on today? _____

_____

_____

_____

_____

_____

_____

What are you thinking, dreaming, praying? _____

_____

_____

_____

_____

_____

_____

_____

_____

_____

God alone made it possible for you to be in Christ Jesus. For our benefit God made Christ to be wisdom itself. He is the one who made us acceptable to God. He made us pure and holy, and he gave himself to purchase our freedom. (1 Corinthians 1:30 NLT)

What stands out? A thought, a word, a phrase. _____

_____

_____

_____

_____

_____

_____

What can be worked on today? _____

_____

_____

_____

_____

_____

What are you thinking, dreaming, praying? _____

_____

_____

_____

_____

_____

_____

_____

_____

Day 96   Proverbs 30   Date: _____

Look carefully then how you walk! Live purposefully and worthily
and accurately, not as the unwise and witless, but as wise (sensible,
intelligent people). (Ephesians 5:15 AMP)

What stands out? A thought, a word, a phrase. _____

_____

_____

_____

_____

_____

_____

What can be worked on today? _____

_____

_____

_____

_____

_____

What are you thinking, dreaming, praying? _____

_____

_____

_____

_____

_____

_____

_____

_____

Day 97   Proverbs 31   Date: _____

You, through Your commandments, make me wiser than my enemies, for [Your words] are ever before me. (Psalms 119:98 AMP)

What stands out? A thought, a word, a phrase. _____

_____

_____

_____

_____

_____

_____

What can be worked on today? _____

_____

_____

_____

_____

_____

_____

What are you thinking, dreaming, praying? _____

_____

_____

_____

_____

_____

_____

_____

_____

_____

_____

One gives freely, yet grows all the richer;
   another withholds what he should give, and only suffers want.
   (Proverbs 11:24 ESV)

What stands out? A thought, a word, a phrase. _____

_____

_____

_____

_____

_____

_____

What can be worked on today? _____

_____

_____

_____

_____

_____

What are you thinking, dreaming, praying? _____

_____

_____

_____

_____

_____

_____

_____

_____

_____

He who tills his land will have plenty of bread,
But he who pursues worthless things lacks sense.
(12:11 NASB)

What stands out? A thought, a word, a phrase. _____

_____

_____

_____

_____

_____

_____

What can be worked on today? _____

_____

_____

_____

_____

_____

_____

What are you thinking, dreaming, praying? _____

_____

_____

_____

_____

_____

_____

_____

_____

Psalms 51:6, 104:24, 111:10, 119:98, I Cor. 1:30

Reckless words pierce like a sword,
but the tongue of the wise brings healing. (12:18 NIV)

What stands out? A thought, a word, a phrase. _____

_____

_____

_____

_____

_____

_____

What can be worked on today? _____

_____

_____

_____

_____

_____

What are you thinking, dreaming, praying? _____

_____

_____

_____

_____

_____

_____

_____

_____

References

Warren, Rick. *The Purpose Driven Life*. Grand Rapids: Zondervan Press, 2002.

Chambers, Oswald. *My Utmost for His Highest*. Uhrichsville: Barbour, 1935.

About the Author

For most of his life Jeff's brothers have accused him of being a full time student. Too many years in school, eleven years working in the family business, and a dozen years in various forms of ministry are the make up of his career. Jeff has served in management, as a Pastor to college students, as an Associate Pastor, as a Senior Pastor and as an Executive Director of a start-up program for abandoned and neglected children.

Today, he is the Director of Upside Down Ministries, Inc. Upside Down Ministries is a non-profit organization that seeks to build and develop healthy relationships through writing, speaking, mentoring and conducting workshops.

He and his wife Libbi have been actively involved with Young Life as volunteer leaders and serving on a Young Life Committee. Jeff and Libbi have been married over 26 years. They have five children: Kristy, Billy, Dickson, Todd and Bo. Home is in Boone, North Carolina.

Need a Speaker?

Click on **www.upsidedownministries.com** for more information about having Jeff Hendley speak to your group or hold a conference or workshop.

Ordering Materials:

You can order materials through the website or contact Jeff Hendley...

Jeff Hendley
Upside Down Ministries, Inc.
PO Box 2567 • Boone, NC 28607
jeff@hendleys.net